MARSE

TRAVEL GUIDE 2024 AND BEYOND

Discover the Hidden Gems of France's Most Vibrant City

JOSEPHINE D. GRIFFIN

All Right Reserved!
No Part of this book may be reproduced, stored in a retrieval system, or transmitted in any form or by any means, electronic or mechanical, photocopying, recording or otherwise, without the prior written permission of the copyright owner
Copyright ©Josephine D. Griffin

TABLE OF CONTENTS

PLANNING YOUR TRIP..2
ACCOMMODATION..2
TOP ATTRACTIONS..2
ACTIVITIES AND EXPERIENCES..2
NEIGHBORHOODS AND DISTRICTS...2

EATING AND DRINKING 2
SHOPPING 2
DAY TRIPS AND EXCURSIONS 2
HISTORY AND CULTURE 2
FAMILY TRAVEL 2
BUDGET ACCOMMODATIONS 2
LGBTQ+ TRAVEL 2
SUSTAINABLE TRAVEL 2
HEALTH AND SAFETY 2
PRACTICAL INFORMATION 2
USEFUL PHRASES AND LANGUAGE GUIDE 2
DIRECTORY 2
BUSINESS AND CONFERENCES 2
SPECIAL INTEREST TRAVEL 2
MARSEILLE ON A BUDGET 2
LOCAL INSIGHTS 2
MARSEILLE ITINERARY 2
CONCLUSION 2
FREQUENTLY ASKED QUESTIONS 2
INTRODUCTION 1

INTRODUCTION

Greetings from Marseille, a vibrant and historically rich city on France's Mediterranean coast. Marseille, is one of the oldest towns in Europe, with a rich history spanning more than 2,600 years.

This thriving port city is well-known for its lively districts, varied cultural offerings, and picturesque coastline vistas. For every tourist, Marseille provides an intriguing experience with its distinctive fusion of the ancient and the contemporary. Marseille's allure is found in its ability to combine modernism with heritage in a seamless manner. **The modern architecture of the MuCEM and other modern monuments contrasts** with the historical streets of the Vieux Port and the medieval Le Panier area.

The city's many museums and galleries provide an abundance of art and history, while its vibrant markets, like the Marché de Noailles, give a flavor of local life and food. **This book is designed to help you discover all Marseille has to offer**. Every segment is intended to assist you in navigating and taking advantage of this dynamic city, ranging from helpful travel advice to in-depth analyses of the city's attractions. This guide will provide all the information you need for an amazing trip to Marseille, whether you're here for a quick visit or a longer stay.

Welcome to Marseille

Welcome to Marseille, a city rich in culture, history, and breathtaking Mediterranean scenery. Marseille is a great place to visit if you're looking for a variety of experiences because of **its compelling fusion of old customs and contemporary conveniences.** Marseille has something to offer everyone in 2024, whether they are lured to its gastronomic pleasures, lively districts, or ancient buildings.

Why Visit Marseille in the Year 2024?

Marseille has a ton of fascinating activities and attractions planned for 2024 that are sure to enthrall tourists from all over the globe. There are plenty of reasons to visit Marseille this year, **from sports events displaying the city's athletic prowess to cultural festivals honoring its rich legacy.** Furthermore, the city's attractions are being enhanced by recent developments and continuing redevelopment initiatives, giving tourists even more options to discover and enjoy.

How to Utilize This Manual

This is your all-in-one guide to Marseille, helping you get the most out of your trip. This book will provide you with **useful knowledge and ideas to improve your trip, regardless of how experienced you are as a traveler.**

Every area has been thoughtfully chosen to include important subjects including travel, lodging, food, sights, and more.

Famous sites like the Basilique Notre-Dame de la Garde, a stunning church with expansive views of the city and the sea, may come into view as you explore Marseille. **The basilica is free to enter**, although contributions are accepted to help with maintenance and upkeep. A trip to the Château d'If is essential for anybody interested in learning more about Marseille's nautical past. You may take a boat from the Vieux Port to this medieval stronghold, which gained notoriety thanks to **Alexandre Dumas'** book **"The Count of Monte Cristo,"** for a little price. Marseille has an array of lodging alternatives to accommodate every budget and taste.

**The InterContinental Marseille - Hotel Dieu, housed in a former hospital and with a view of the Vieux Port, is a wonderful place to stay. Reservations for rooms may be made online or by phone at +33 4 13 42 42

42, with pricing starting at $250 per night. Hostels near the city center, such as Vertigo Vieux-Port, provide reasonably priced lodging for those on a tight budget. Reservations for dorm beds may be made by email at info@vertigo-marseille.com; rates begin at $30 per night.

Food enthusiasts will enjoy exploring Marseille's culinary scene, which has a wide variety of eateries and cafés serving mouthwatering cuisine from all over the globe. In the Vallon des Auffes district, try Chez Fonfon for a taste of authentic Provencal food. This little restaurant, which specializes in fish delicacies like bouillabaisse, has prix-fixe meals that start at $50 per person. Making reservations by phone at +33 4 91 52 14 38 or email at contact@chez-fonfon.com is advised. **Use this book as your reliable travel companion** as you set out to discover Marseille's hidden treasures and life-changing adventures.

Marseille is certain to make an imprint on your heart and mind, whether you want to explore its historical sites, indulge in its delectable cuisine, or just take in its lively environment.

PLANNING YOUR TRIP

To guarantee a hassle-free and pleasurable journey, planning a trip to Marseille requires taking into account several elements. **Here is a thorough guide to help you plan your trip efficiently, from determining the ideal time to visit to selecting your mode of transportation.**

Best Time to Visit

The ideal time to visit Marseille may depend on your tastes and objectives. **The city has scorching summers and mild winters due to its Mediterranean environment.** For favorable weather and fewer people, spring **(April to June) and autumn (September to October)** are the best seasons for outdoor activities and sightseeing. The busiest travel season, however, is summer **(July to August),** when there are many festivals and concerts along busy roadways.

How to Get to Marseille

Travelers have a variety of ways to get to Marseille, including plane, rail, automobile, and marine transportation.

By Air: The primary airport servicing the city is **Marseille Provence Airport (MRS),** which is situated about 27 kilometers northwest of the city center. **The airport connects Marseille to major cities in Europe and beyond with both local and international flights.** To get to the city center from the airport, visitors may use rental vehicles, taxis, or airport shuttles.

By Train: Marseille has a wide rail network that connects it to other French and European cities. Numerous train stations service the city, the major one being Marseille Saint-Charles, which is situated in the heart of the city. **Travelers coming from Paris, Lyon, Nice, and other locations** have access to effective transit alternatives via high-speed trains like the TGV and regional trains.

By Car: Driving a car to Marseille allows you freedom and convenience, particularly if you want to explore the Provence area that surrounds Marseille. **Marseille is connected to Lyon, Nice, and Montpellier via major roadways such as the A7 and A50.** But parking in the city center might be difficult due to traffic congestion, so it's best to park your vehicle in approved spots and use public transit to go about the city.

By Sea: The Vieux Port, Marseille's ancient port is open to cruise ships and ferry services from other Mediterranean locations. When traveling by boat, visitors may simply disembark at the port and use public transit or foot to get to the city center.

Navigating Marseille

Once you're in Marseille, navigating the city is somewhat simple because of its effective public transit system and various alternatives.

Public Transportation: Marseille has an extensive public transit system that includes metro lines, trams, and buses. These services are run by the RTM (Régie des Transports de Marseille), and they provide easy access to major landmarks, residential areas, and suburbs.

Single tickets and multi-day: passes are available for purchase at ticket machines or specific locations. Both ride-sharing and taxis In Marseille, taxis are widely accessible and may be reserved ahead of time or called on the street.

Furthermore, ride-sharing services like Uber function inside the city, providing an additional practical means of transportation.

Biking and Walking: Discovering Marseille by bicycle or foot is an excellent method to take in the lively ambiance and breathtaking scenery of the city. It is safe and pleasant to ride a bike or take a walk around the city thanks to its bike lanes and pedestrian-friendly zones. Bicycles may be rented for a short or long period from several firms, letting tourists see Marseille at their leisure.

Travel Advice and Useful Information

Before you go to Marseille, have in mind the following important advice and useful information.

Terminology and Handy: ExpressionsIn Marseille, the official language is French, however, English is often understood in institutions and tourist areas.

Acquiring some basic French language skills will improve your trip experience and make it easier for you to interact with locals.

Currency and Banking: The Euro (EUR) is the official currency of France. There are plenty of **ATMs in Marseille that let visitors get cash using debit or credit cards.** Most hotels, restaurants, and stores accept major credit cards, but for minor purchases and transactions, it's recommended to have some cash on hand.

Safety and Health: Although Marseille is a fairly secure city for tourists, you should always take common-sense safety measures. Be mindful of your surroundings, safeguard your possessions, and avoid going on long walks in remote places, particularly after dark. Should an emergency arise, **contact 112 in Europe for help.**

Availability: While Marseille is making efforts to make its tourist attractions more accessible to people with disabilities, some obstacles could still be present, particularly in older structures and historic sites. **Accessible rooms and amenities are available at many hotels, restaurants, and public transit stops;** nevertheless, it's best to check beforehand to make sure your requirements will be satisfied while there. **In addition, there are several institutions and organizations in Marseille that provide help and support to visitors with impairments.**

ACCOMMODATION

Selecting the ideal lodging option is essential to making the most of your vacation to Marseille. To assist you in making an educated choice, this section gives you an overview of the many areas and lodging options.

Overview of Neighborhoods

Marseille is home to a variety of areas, each with its vibe and selection of lodging options. This is a list of some of the most well-liked locations that you may want to stay in.

Vieux Port: Port VieuxMarseille's center, known as the Vieux Port (Old Port), is a hive of activity. For people who want to live close to the action, this neighborhood is great since it offers quick access to eateries, bars, stores, and popular attractions.

Another fantastic location to take in stunning views of the port and the Mediterranean Sea is the Vieux Port.

Le Panier: Marseille's oldest neighborhood, Le Panier, is distinguished by its meandering, tiny alleyways, vibrant architecture, and creative atmosphere. You may experience a little bit of the rich history and culture of the city by lodging in this historic district. It is a delightful area to stroll about on foot since it is home to several artisan stores, galleries, and cozy cafés.

La Corniche: La Corniche is a charming seaside neighborhood with breathtaking views of the Mediterranean. This area is ideal for anyone seeking a more tranquil, scenic environment. La Corniche is a great option for beach enthusiasts since it has some of the nicest beaches in the city.

La Plaine and Cours Julien: La Plaine and Cours Julien are renowned for their free-spirited, creative vibe. Younger tourists and those seeking lively nightlife are drawn to this region. Street art, music venues, and hip pubs abound, fostering an energetic and imaginative atmosphere.

Prado and Périer: Périer and Prado Upscale residential areas Prado and Périer provide a more calm and elegant environment. These neighborhoods are well-known for their parks, classy boulevards, and easy access to the beach. Families and visitors looking for a more tranquil stay near the city center will find it to be an excellent option.

Accommodation Types

Marseille has a variety of lodging choices, from luxurious hotels to inexpensive hostels, to fit every taste and budget.

Hotels: Accommodation hotels in Marseille range widely in price from low-cost to high-end. Here are some suggestions:

InterContinental Marseille - Hotel Dieu: This opulent hotel provides tasteful cuisine, a spa, and magnificent rooms all set in a beautifully renovated 18th-century edifice with a view of the Vieux Port. Starting prices are around €250 per night. Reservations may be booked by phone at +33 4 13 42 42 42 or online.

NH Collection Marseille: This contemporary hotel offers cozy accommodations, a restaurant, and a fitness facility. It is located in the La Joliette neighborhood. Starting prices are around €100 per night. Online reservations or phone calls at +33 4 91 99 33 33 are accepted.

Hotel Hermès: A cheap choice close to the Vieux Port, with straightforward, tidy rooms and a nice rooftop patio with views. Starting prices are around €60 per night. Online reservations or phone calls at +33 4 96 11 63 63 are accepted.

Hostels: Hostels In Marseille, hostels provide social and reasonably priced lodging for those on a tight budget.

Vertigo Vieux-Port: This well-liked hostel has a common kitchen, a bar, and both private and dorm bedrooms. Dormitory bed rates begin at €25 per night. Reservations may be sent to info@vertigo-marseille.com via email.

The People Hostel Marseille is a hostel with a combination of private and dorm rooms, a bar, and a patio that is close to the Saint-Charles train station. Dormitory bed rates begin at €20 per night. You may make reservations by phone at +33 4 65 85 00 90 or online.

Vacation Rentals and Apartments: Hiring a vacation house or apartment may be a terrific way to have additional room and a more homey feel. Airbnb: Provides a large selection of houses and flats in different districts, ranging from affordable alternatives to opulent villas. The nature and location of the property affect the price.

Marseille Apartment Euromed Provides fully furnished apartments with kitchenettes, excellent for extended stays. Starting prices are around €50 per night. Online reservations or phone calls at +33 4 91 00 08 70 are accepted.

Options for Boutique and LuxuryIn addition: Marseille has several upscale and boutique hotels for visitors seeking a more upscale experience. The C2 Hotel is a boutique hotel with modern amenities including a bar and spa that is set in a 19th-century mansion. Starting prices are around €180 per night. Reservations may be booked by phone at **+33 4 95 05 13 13, or online.**

Le)Petit Nice Passedat is a five-star hotel and restaurant on the coast that offers gourmet food and breathtaking views of the sea. Starting prices are around €300 per night. Online reservations or phone calls at +33 4 91 59 25 92 are accepted.

Recommended Accommodations

Here are some excellent suggestions for lodging in Marseille that suit a range of tastes and price ranges.

Regarding Luxuriousness: The historical charm, first-rate services, and ideal position close to the Vieux Port make the InterContinental Marseille - Hotel Dieu a great option.

For Mid-Range: The NH Collection Marseille is the perfect choice for both business and leisure visitors since it has contemporary amenities, is conveniently located, and is reasonably priced.

On a Budget: Hotel Hermès offers reasonably priced lodging along with the perk of a rooftop terrace with views of the Vieux Port.

Regarding Hostels: Due to its convenient location, welcoming ambiance, and reasonable prices, Vertigo Vieux-Port is a top choice for travelers.

For Boutique Rentals: The C2 Hotel offers a magnificent but cozy experience, standing out for its distinctive fusion of modern and ancient architecture. When it comes to vacation rentals, Airbnb has a wide range of options, so visitors may choose the ideal place to stay, **whether they'd rather rent a coastal house in La Corniche or a cozy apartment in Le Panier.**

With the help of our comprehensive guide to Marseille lodging alternatives, you may choose the ideal location for your needs in terms of preferences, price range, and kind of experience. **Have fun while visiting this energetic and ancient city!**

TOP ATTRACTIONS

Marseille is a captivating city with a wealth of natural beauty, history, and culture. It also has a lot to offer tourists. These are some of the best attractions you shouldn't miss, ranging from contemporary museums to historic sites.

Port Vieux

Every tourist must see the Vieux Port, often known as the **Old Port,** which is the center of Marseille. Since ancient times, it has been the vibrant center of the city's marine activity and continues to attract both residents and visitors. **The port is a bustling place for eating and recreation since it is surrounded by eateries, cafés, and retail establishments.** Enjoy delicious seafood at a waterfront restaurant, walk around the quays at a leisurely pace, or just gaze out at the breathtaking views of the sea and boats. Location: 13002 Marseille.

Basilique Notre-Dame de la Garde

Quai du PortEntry Not Charged Hours Available around-the-clock Notre-Dame de la Garde.

Basilique Marseille: The most famous landmark is the Basilique Notre-Dame de la Garde, which is perched on the city's tallest hill. Known as **"La Bonne Mère"** (The Good Mother), this magnificent church provides expansive views over Marseille and the Mediterranean. The basilica, which dates back to the 1800s, has a figure of the Virgin Mary, stunning mosaics, and a remarkable bell tower. It is a popular tourist destination as well as a site of pilgrimage. Fort du Sanctuaire, **13281 Marseille is the address**.

Free admission; donations accepted hours are 7:00 AM to 6:15 PM. Phone: (33 4) 91-13-40 80

MuCEM (Museum of European and Mediterranean Civilisations)

Museum of European and Mediterranean Civilizations, or MuCEM for short the entrance to the Vieux Port stands the contemporary architectural wonder that is the MuCEM. This museum uses a wide range of exhibits, such as historical objects, photography, and artwork, to examine the cultures and histories of the Mediterranean area.

The MuCEM is a unique attraction due to its remarkable architecture, which includes a latticework facade and breathtaking sea vistas. For amazing views of the port and the ocean, don't miss the rooftop patio. **Location: 13002 Marseille, 7 Prom. Robert Laffont.**

Entry fee: €9.50 (full fare), €5 (discounted).Hours: 10:00 AM - 7:00 PM, every day except Tuesdays.Phone: (334) 84-35-13

District of Le Panier: The oldest district in Marseille, Le Panier, is renowned for its charming, twisting lanes, vibrant architecture, and creative atmosphere. With its quaint squares, old buildings, and colorful street art, **Le Panier** is like traveling back in time. **La Vieille Charité**, a converted almshouse into a cultural center, and the many artisan stores and cafés are the district's main attractions.

13002 Marseille is the location. Admission: Free to explore; some sites have an admission charge hours.

Available around-the-clockChâteau d'If: Situated on the Île d'If, a short distance from Marseille's shore, lies the medieval fortification known as Château d'If. The castle, which became well-known via Alexandre Dumas' book **"The Count of Monte Cristo,"** was used as a jail for many years. Today, guests may take in breathtaking views of the

Mediterranean, tour its meticulously conserved cells, and discover its history. Regular ferries from the Vieux Port go to the island. Location: 13007 Marseille, Île d'IfAdult admission is €6, children are €5. **Daily hours are 10:00 AM to 6:00 PM.** **(Season-specific hours vary)Phone: (33 4) 91-59-02-30**

Longchamp Palace

The Natural History Museum and the Musée des Beaux-Arts are housed in the magnificent architectural complex known as the Palais Longchamp. **Constructed during the 1800s, the palace is well-known for its striking fountain, imposing colonnades, and exquisitely designed gardens**. Artworks by French and Italian painters may be seen at the Musée des Beaux-Arts, while intriguing displays on fossils, geology, and ethnology can be found at the Natural History Museum.

Address: 13004 Marseille, Boulevard Jardin ZoologiqueAdmission: €6 for adults, €0 for minors, and free on Sundays

Hours: 9:00 AM to 7:00 PM, Tuesday through Sunday.

Phone: (33 4) 91-14-59-50

The Old Charity In the center of the Le Panier neighborhood stands the famous La Vieille Charité. Built as an almshouse in the seventeenth century, it is now a cultural hub with many museums and exhibition spaces. **With a chapel and a central courtyard,** the structure is a masterwork of Baroque design. The Museum of African, Oceanian, and Amerindian Arts and the Museum of Mediterranean Archaeology include important displays.

Location: 13002 Marseille, 2 Rue de la.

CharitéEntry: Depends on the show; usually between €6 and €8)Open from Tuesday to Sunday. 10:00 A.M. to 6:00 P.M.Phone: (33 4) 91-14-58 80

Parc BorélyLarge public park Parc Borély provides a tranquil haven from the bustle of the city. Beautiful gardens may be found in the park, including a botanical garden, an English landscape garden, and a French formal garden. A lake with playgrounds for kids, strolling and cycling routes, and boat rentals is another attraction for visitors. The Museum of Decorative Arts, Fashion, and Ceramics is housed at the Château

Borély, which is located inside the park.

Location: 13008 Marseille, Avenue du Prado.

Admission: Free (but certain park attractions may charge an admission fee)Hours: 6:00 AM to 9:00 PM, every day **Phone: (334) 91-55-25-51**

National Park of Calanques Not far from Marseille is the natural beauty known as the Calanques National Park. The striking limestone cliffs, turquoise waves, and secluded coves of this untamed coastal region have made it renowned. Numerous recreational pursuits are available in the park, including swimming, kayaking, rock climbing, and hiking. Within the park, the Calanques de Sormiou, Morgiou, and d'En-Vau are well-liked locations. For those who like the outdoors and want adventure, this place is perfect.

Address: 13009 Marseille.

Admission: Free (activities and guided tours may incur expenses)

Hours: Open 24/7 (summer access may be limited owing to fire danger)Phone: (334) 20-10-50-00

In summary: Marseille has a diverse range of attractions, including its historic port, medieval districts, contemporary museums, and lush natural parks. Marseille has plenty to offer, regardless of your interests—history, art, the outdoors, or just taking in the energetic environment. **To get the most out of your trip to this intriguing Mediterranean city, be sure to include these top sites in your schedule.**

ACTIVITIES AND EXPERIENCES

There are plenty of exciting things to do and see in Marseille for all kinds of tourists. There is something for everyone to enjoy, from sun-kissed beaches and exhilarating water sports to cultural excursions and mouth watering cuisine.

Water Sports and Beaches

Both sun worshippers and thrill seekers can find plenty of beaches and water sports along Marseille's coastline.

Best Beaches Plage des Catalans: This sandy beach is well-known for its vibrant environment and proximity to the Vieux Port, both of which are in the city center. It's ideal for beach volleyball and swimming.

Plage du Prado: A group of beaches with plenty of space, playgrounds, and picnic spaces that are located along the Prado Seaside Park. Families and people wishing to unwind by the shore will love it.

Plage de la Pointe Rouge: A sandy beach with crystal-clear seas and cafés along the shore, situated in Marseille's southern region. Perfect for dining al fresco and swimming.

Boating and Sailing: Marseille is a great place for boaters and sailors because of its coastal position. Numerous businesses provide guided tours, sailing excursions, and boat rentals.

SailEasy: All skill levels may hire boats and take sailing lessons with SailEazy. They have a variety of boats, from tiny sailboats to bigger yachts, and are situated near the Vieux Port. The kind of boat and length of hire affect the cost.

For bookings, call +33 7 68 02 87 14 or go to their website.

Blue Boats: Provides expertly guided boat trips along the coast, which include stops at the Calanques. Tours provide the chance to swim in pristine waters and discover secret coves. The starting price per person is €45. **Please**

contact **+33 6 46 18 17 89 for more details.**

Snorkeling and Scuba Diving: The Mediterranean's crystal-clear waters provide perfect snorkeling and scuba diving locations. Numerous diving facilities and schools in Marseille provide instruction and guided dives.

Academia: A diving school that provides guided dives in the Calanques National Park along with a variety of courses for all skill levels. Beginner classes are priced starting at €60. **For bookings and more information, visit their website or call +33 6 80 73 24 21.**

Plongée Passion: This diving shop, which is close to the Vieux Port, provides advanced training, basic dives, and snorkeling excursions. Snorkeling excursions begin at €30 per person. For appointments, call +33 4 91 52 46 99.

Outside Activities

Marseille has a wide range of outdoor activities, like hiking, walking tours, and cycling, for people who enjoy on-land experiences.

Walking & Hiking Tours: The varied topography of Marseille offers many chances for hiking and walking excursions. Hiking aficionados consider the Calanques National Park to be a great destination.

The routes in Calanques: National Park range in difficulty from short strolls to strenuous treks. One of the most well-liked hikes is Calanque d'En-Vau, which provides stunning views of the sea and rocks.

No-cost Walking Tours Marseille: Offers both famous and obscure gem-guided walking tours across the city. Although the tour is free, tips are welcome. For meeting locations and scheduling, see their website.

Routes for Cycling Cycling, is a fantastic way to see Marseille and the surrounding area. There are several bike-friendly paths throughout the city that are suitable for riders of all skill levels.

Corniche Kennedy: A charming coastal path that provides breathtaking views of the Mediterranean. This is an all-level course that is rather flat.

Prado Seaside Park has a system of bike lanes that wind through the park and by the beaches, making it an ideal place to ride slowly.

Cultural Encounters: Marseille has an abundant cultural landscape that encompasses museums, art galleries, music, performing arts, and lively festivals and events held all year round. **Museums and Galleries of Art Numerous museums and art galleries displaying a vast array of artwork and historical items can be found in Marseille.**

Art Galleries and Museums: This museum, which is housed in Palais Longchamp, has a sizable collection of European sculptures and paintings. Entry fee: €6. **Please contact +33 4 91 14 59 50 for more details.**

MAC (Musée d'Art Contemporain): Presents a changing collection of modern artists' artwork with an emphasis on contemporary art. Entry fee: €9. For information, **call +33 4 91 25 01 07**. The Performing Arts and MusicMarseille has a thriving performing arts and music scene, with a wide range of events taking place in many locations. Opéra de Marseille presents a wide range of concerts, ballets, and operas all year round. Their website has the schedule and tickets.

For bookings, call +33 4 91 55 11 10.

Le Silo: A multipurpose space that hosts plays, concerts, and other cultural gatherings. For information about future concerts and tickets, see their website.

Events and Festivals in 2024 Marseille celebrates its rich cultural past and diversity with several festivals and events.

Festival de Marseille: An outdoor summer event including performances of modern dance, theater, and music. held at several locations across the city. Tickets and dates are listed on their website. **Every year on June 21, the city comes alive with free concerts and entertainment during Fête de la Musique. An excellent method to hear music from across the world and locally.**

Culinary Experiences

For many tourists, one of the highlights of Marseille is its gastronomic scene, which provides an opportunity to sample and learn about the regional cuisine. Cooking Courses

Cooking Classes: A great method to get familiar with Provençal food and learn how to prepare traditional meals is to enroll in a cooking class. The hands-on culinary workshops at L'Atelier des Chefs teach you how to make aioli and bouillabaisse. The first lesson costs €60 per student. Reservations and class schedules may be found on their website or by **calling +33 4 91 53 03 44.**

Les Apprentis Gourmets: Offers cooking classes with an emphasis on regional cuisine and in-season ingredients. The starting price per person is €50. Please contact +33 4 91 47 79 74 for more details.

Tours of Food and Wine: Take advantage of guided food and wine excursions that take you to the greatest local markets, restaurants, and vineyards to discover Marseille's gastronomic treasures.

Marseille Gastronomy excursions: Provides guided food excursions that include the history of the city's cuisine, traditional restaurant tastings, and trips to local markets. The starting price per person is €75.

For appointments, call +33 4 91 87 77 77.

Provence Wine Tours offers day visits to surrounding vineyards so you may sample a range of Provençal wines and see how they're made. The starting price per person is €95. **Please call +33 4 94 90 86 82** for bookings and more information.

In summary: Marseille has a diverse range of experiences and activities to suit every taste, from lounging on the beach and discovering underwater worlds to trekking picturesque paths and indulging in delectable cuisine. **Marseille has something to offer everyone, whether they are foodies, cultural vultures, or thrill seekers.** To get the most out of your stay in this energetic Mediterranean city, **arrange your schedule to incorporate these varied experiences and activities.**

NEIGHBORHOODS AND DISTRICTS

Marseille is a city of many districts and neighborhoods, each with its distinct history, culture, and points of interest. Here's a tour of some of Marseille's most famous districts, from the lively Vieux Port to the creative haven of Le Panier.

Vieux Port

Marseille's Central DistrictMarseille's historic and cultural center is the Vieux Port, often known as the Old Port. This busy waterfront, which dates back to antiquity, has long served as the center of the city's activities. It is still a thriving center for business, recreation, and tourism today.

Attractions

Watch vessels arrive and go from the port, and watch fishermen unload their daily haul.

Quayside Cafés: Unwind at one of the numerous eateries and cafés along the waterfront while savoring pastis and views of the busy port.

Fort Saint-Jean: Explore the storied Fort Saint-Jean, which stands watch over the port's entrance and provides sweeping views of the surrounding area and the ocean.

Accommodation

InterContinental Marseille - Hotel Dieu: An opulent lodging with exquisite views and first-rate facilities situated on the edge of the Vieux Port.Le Panier: Artist and HistorianThe oldest district in Marseille, Le Panier, is renowned for its charming cobblestone lanes, vibrant façade, and creative flair. For creatives such as designers and painters, this bohemian oasis offers a sanctuary.

Attractions: La Vieille Charité: Explore this converted almshouse that is now a cultural hub with galleries, museums, and exhibition spaces.

Street Art: Explore Le Panier's streets to find eye-catching murals and other works of street art.

Boutique Shops: Peruse the many ateliers and stores offering jewelry, clothing, and handcrafted items.

Accommodations: Hotel Hermes: Located in the center of Le Panier, this affordable hotel offers cozy lodgings and quick access to the area's attractions.

La Corniche: Enchanting and CalmA charming seaside neighborhood, La Corniche is well-known for its breathtaking views of the Mediterranean and the recognizable Château d'If. This charming neighborhood provides a tranquil escape from the bustle of the city center.

Points of interest: Corniche Kennedy: Enjoy a leisurely walk along this picturesque seaside boulevard, which provides expansive views of the city and the sea.

Plage des Catalans: Unwind on this sandy beach, which is well-liked by both residents and visitors and take pleasure in swimming in the Mediterranean's crystal-clear blue waves.

A place to stay: A five-star establishment with tasteful accommodations and stunning views of the ocean, situated along the Kennedy Corniche.

La Plaine and Cours Julien

A Bohemian Feeling The dynamic areas of Cours Julien and La Plaine are well-known for their colorful street art, bohemian vibe, and exciting nightlife. Students, musicians, and artists love to hang out at this creative haven.

Attractions

Street Art: Discover a variety of murals, graffiti, and creative installations by strolling through the vibrant streets of Cours Julien and La Plaine.

Cafés and Bars: Take advantage of the numerous trendy cafés, bars, and restaurants in the area for a meal or a drink. numerous of them have live music performances by DJs.

Accommodations:

Hotel C2: Hotel C2 is a boutique hotel with chic rooms and a rooftop pool with expansive city views that is close to Cours Julien.

Périer and Prado: Elegant LivingUpmarket residential areas Prado and Périer are renowned for their tasteful architecture, verdant boulevards, and first-rate facilities. Rich residential areas provide a tranquil escape from the city center, yet Marseille's attractions are still easily accessible from these areas.

Attractions

Take a stroll or have a picnic in this vast park that has lakes, walking routes, and botanical gardens.

Shopping: Peruse the high-end boutiques and designer shops along Avenue du Prado, which provide an extensive selection of clothing, jewelry, and home furnishings.

Accommodations

Marseille's Radisson Blu Hotel Located in the Prado neighborhood, Vieux Port is a five-star hotel with contemporary lodging with expansive views of the city and the ocean.

L'Estaque: Creative BeachfrontA charming beach town on Marseille's outskirts is called L'Estaque. Artists such as Paul Cézanne and Georges Braque have drawn inspiration from this little area for a long time.

Attractions

Wander down this waterfront promenade, which is dotted with cafés, art studios, and galleries where you can take in the breathtaking views of the sea and local artwork.

Visit the Château de l'Estaque, a medieval castle that is now home to a cultural center and an exhibition area with modern and contemporary photography and art.

Place to Stay: Villa Blanche The Estaque: In the center of L'Estaque, this little bed & breakfast provides warm lodgings and attentive service.

In summary, the historic appeal of the Vieux Port to the creative enclave of Le Panier, **the panoramic beauty of La Corniche, and the bohemian vibes of Cours Julien and La Plaine, Marseille's numerous neighborhoods and districts have something to offer every kind of tourist.**

Marseille offers a neighborhood to fit your tastes and style, whether you're searching for premium elegance, a tranquil beach getaway, or a cultural experience. **Discover the city's rich history, culture, and scenic beauty by exploring its lively areas.**

EATING AND DRINKING

Food lovers will find a veritable rainbow of tastes and

gastronomic adventures in Marseille. Your taste buds will be delighted by the city's diversified eating scene, which features both international and traditional Provençal food.

Overview of Marseille Cuisine

Marseille's rich cultural legacy and maritime setting are reflected in the city's gastronomy. Fresh fish, fragrant herbs, and robust tastes define Marseille's culinary offerings, which are influenced by Provençal traditions and Mediterranean cuisines.

Essential Components: Marseille has an abundance of fresh seafood, including fish, shellfish, and crustaceans, because of its closeness to the Mediterranean Sea. Olive Oil: A mainstay of Provençal cookery, Marseille cuisine makes liberal use of olive oil to accentuate tastes and textures.

Herbs: Many Marseille meals benefit from the richness and smell of Herbes de Provence, a combination of fragrant herbs including oregano, thyme, and rosemary.

Must-Try Recipes Without trying some of Marseille's specialty foods, which highlight the city's culinary skills and rich cultural legacy, a trip there wouldn't be complete.

Bouillabaisse: Marseille is the home of bouillabaisse, a substantial fish stew cooked with a variety of fish, crustaceans, tomatoes, onions, garlic, and fragrant herbs. A favorite local dish that perfectly captures the aromas of the Mediterranean, bouillabaisse is traditionally served with crusty bread and rouille, a mayonnaise flavored with garlic.

Aioli: Traditionally prepared with garlic, olive oil, and egg yolk, aioli is a Provençal sauce that tastes a lot like mayonnaise but with a stronger garlic taste. It is often used as a spread for toast or as a dip for boiling vegetables and shellfish.

Pastis: Popular in Marseille and across Provence, pastis is a liquor with an anise taste. Pastis is often drunk as an aperitif, diluted with water to unleash its full taste and cause it to become hazy. This cool beverage is particularly well-liked in the sweltering summer months.

Navettes: Traditionally enjoyed during religious holidays such as Candlemas and Easter, navettes are little biscuits fashioned like boats. Both residents and tourists love these crispy cookies, which are made with orange blossom water and flavored with lemon zest.

Fine Dining: Chef Gérald Passedat's three-Michelin-starred Le Petit Nice Passedat provides a remarkable dining experience with a view of the Mediterranean. Renowned for its inventive seafood preparations and flawless service, Le Petit Nice Passedat is a gastronomic treasure that should not be overlooked.

Mid-Range Choices: Nestled in the Vallon des Auffes area, Chez Fonfon is a well-loved Marseille institution that serves up fresh fish and classic bouillabaisse. Residents as well as tourists love the restaurant for its quaint surroundings and friendly service.

Budget Bits: Le Marché des Enfants Rouges: This lively indoor market in the Le Panier neighborhood provides reasonably priced foreign food. You may discover a wide variety of cuisines and foods to sate your appetites, from Japanese sushi to Moroccan tagines.

Bakeries and Cafés

Marseille has a thriving café culture that permeates every aspect of everyday life. The city is home to a large number of cafés and bakeries where residents congregate to mingle, have a leisurely dinner, or just enjoy a pastry and a cup of coffee.

Coffee shops: l'Abbaye Café A little café with a lovely outside patio, Café de l'Abbaye is tucked away in the center of the Le Panier area. Enjoying a morning cappuccino or an afternoon glass of wine while taking in the atmosphere of this ancient quarter is the ideal way to unwind here. Bakeries:

La Mie Caline: With many sites across Marseille, this well-known chain of bakeries serves a delectable assortment of freshly baked bread, pastries, and sandwiches. La Mie Caline caters to your need for both flaky croissants and crusty baguettes. Pubs and After-Dark ActivitiesMarseille has a thriving nightlife culture that suits all interests and inclinations after dark. There are many alternatives to keep you occupied until the wee hours of the morning, whether you're in the mood for live music, a handmade cocktail, or a glass of wine.

Wine Bars

This little wine bar in the Vieux Port neighborhood specializes in natural and organic wines from local growers.

You may choose the ideal bottle of wine to go with your dinner by navigating the large wine selection with the assistance of the expert staff.
Cocktail Bars:

Le Bar de la Marine: This chic cocktail bar with breathtaking sea views is located on the Corniche Kennedy. As you take in live music or DJ sets, savor professionally created cocktails created with quality alcohol and fresh ingredients.

Live Music Locations: Live music is offered all week long at this unique pub and music venue in the Cours Julien district, including local bands and DJs. Discover new music and have a great time dancing at Molotov, which has a varied audience and a laid-back vibe.

In summary: Discover a wide variety of sensations and experiences in Marseille's thriving culinary scene, which is a feast for the senses. The city's diverse gastronomic offerings, which include pastis and navettes as well as classic Provençal fare like bouillabaisse and aioli, will leave you wanting more. **Marseille has options for every taste and preference,** whether you're eating at a restaurant with a Michelin star, having a leisurely dinner at a local cafe, or sipping drinks at a hip bar. So treat your palate and discover **Marseille's delights - bon appétit!**

SHOPPING

With a wide variety of shopping experiences available, including lively markets, chic shops, and pedestrian retail districts, Marseille is a shoppers' paradise. Marseille has plenty to offer any kind of consumer, whether they are looking for high-end couture, distinctive gifts, or regional specialties.

Markets

Residents and tourists alike congregate in Marseille's markets, which are hive centers of activity, to purchase fresh vegetables, handcrafted crafts, and one-of-a-kind finds.

These three marketplaces in Marseille are a must-see

Noailles Marché: Nestled in the cosmopolitan Noailles district, the lively Marché de Noailles is renowned for its wide selection of global goods. You may discover a vast variety of things that entice your senses, from fresh fruits and vegetables to exotic spices and Middle Eastern delicacies. Don't pass up the chance to try regional delicacies like freshly squeezed juices and North African sweets.

Marché du Prado: One of Marseille's biggest and most well-liked marketplaces, it is located next to the Parc Chanot conference center. This expansive market, spanning many blocks, provides a wide range of products, including apparel, home items, fresh fish and meats, and much more. While you browse the booths and look for deals and gems, strike up a conversation with the merchants and take in the vibrant environment.

Marché des Capucins: Located in the center of the Vieux Port neighborhood, this quaint market is well-known for its vibrant displays of fresh produce, flowers, fruits, and regional delicacies. Discover handmade cheeses, cured meats, seasonal fruits, and other gourmet treats by perusing the booths. Don't forget to have a glass of wine at one of the lively cafés in the market or try some freshly shucked oysters.

Streets and Districts for Shopping: Marseille has a variety of lively retail areas and streets in addition to its markets, where you can find everything from upscale clothing to unique boutiques and handcrafted stores.

La Canebiere: Marseille's most well-known avenue, La Canebière, is dotted with boutiques, cafés, and old buildings. This busy street is the ideal location to buy clothing, souvenirs, and regional goods while taking in the vibrant ambiance.

Take advantage of the chance to explore the side streets and lanes that lead off from La Canebière; you'll come across interesting discoveries and hidden treasures. The primary shopping district of Marseille, Rue Saint-Ferréol is dotted with a variety of boutiques, department stores, and retail establishments.

Rue Saint-Ferréol: Rue Saint-Ferréol has everything you could want, whether you're searching for designer labels, chic accessories, or reasonably priced mementos. Enjoy a leisurely walk down this busy street, pausing to look around the stores and have a snack or coffee at one of the cafés along the route.

Les Terrasses du Port: Located on Marseille's waterfront, Les Terrasses du Port is a contemporary retail area with a variety of local and international brands, eateries, and entertainment venues. Les Terrasses du Port, with its gorgeous architecture and waterfront setting, is the ideal spot to shop, eat, and unwind while admiring the Mediterranean Sea.

Keepsakes and Regional Items

Getting some local goods and mementos to take home would make any vacation to Marseille complete. Here are three souvenirs that perfectly capture Marseille's essence:

Marseille soap: Known for its natural ingredients and mild washing capabilities, Marseille soap is a local specialty. Marseille soap is made from olive oil, palm oil, and soda ash. It comes in a range of forms and flavors, making it the ideal present for friends and family back home or as a keepsake.

Provençal Textiles: With its vivid hues and classic designs that capture the allure and magnificence of the Provence area, Provençal textiles are yet another well-liked option for souvenirs. Look for kitchen towels, tablecloths, and napkins with traditional Provençal patterns like lavender fields, sunflowers, and olives.

Local Wines and Spirits: Marseille is the ideal location to purchase a bottle of wine or spirits to enjoy during your visit or bring home as a memento since it is encircled by some of France's most renowned wine districts. Seek out wines from neighboring appellations such as Bandol and Côtes de Provence, along with regional liqueurs like pastis and absinthe.

In summary: Marseille's vivid marketplaces, busy retail avenues, and quaint shops providing a vast array of goods to fit every taste and price make shopping there a sensory joy. **Marseille has something for everyone, whether you're looking for handcrafted items, fresh fruit, or distinctive gifts.** Thus, take your time, peruse the many retail offerings of the city, **and carry home a memento of Marseille that you will always treasure.**

DAY TRIPS AND EXCURSIONS

Although there are many sights and things to do in Marseille, the Provence area is just as rich in natural beauty, history, and culture. From Marseille, one may enjoy a plethora of day trips and excursions to breathtaking coastal

scenery and quaint towns. **The following six locations are must-sees:**
Aix-en-Provence

Aix-en-Provence, a lovely city renowned for its exquisite architecture, quaint streets, and lively cultural scene, is just a short drive from Marseille. **Aix-en-Provence, the birthplace of post-impressionist painter Paul Cézanne, is home to a plethora of museums, galleries, and buildings honoring its creative legacy.** In addition to seeing the ancient Old Town and taking in sights like the Saint-Sauveur Cathedral and Cézanne Studio, visitors may meander along the verdant Cours Mirabeau. Savor the delectable pastries, chocolates, and crisp local wines that Aix has to offer; don't pass this up.

Calanques and Cassis: Cassis is a quaint fishing community tucked between stunning limestone cliffs and the glittering Mediterranean Sea, just a short drive south of Marseille. **The town's charming port** is the ideal location for a leisurely seafood lunch or a boat tour of the breathtaking Calanques National Park since it is dotted with vibrant buildings and lively eateries.

These untamed limestone fjords have clean waters that are perfect for swimming, snorkeling, and trekking, and they provide some of France's most beautiful coastline landscapes. Cassis will enthrall you with its natural beauty and laid-back vibe whether you're strolling through the town streets or lounging on a remote beach.

Avignon: An hour's drive northwest of Marseille lies Avignon, a **UNESCO World Heritage** site recognized for its rich history and well-preserved medieval architecture. The Palais des Papes, a vast fortress-palace that housed the popes in the fourteenth century, is the city's most famous feature. Explore the palace's great halls, gardens, and chapels.

You can also take a leisurely walk around the old city walls to get sweeping views of the Rhône River and the surrounding landscape. Another well-known feature of Avignon is its yearly summertime performing arts festival, which draws spectators and performers from all over the globe.

Arles: a picturesque Provencal town on the banks of the Rhône River, is well-known for its Roman remains, ties to Van Gogh, and thriving arts and culture scene. Wander through the beautifully preserved Roman amphitheater, take a leisurely walk along the scenic Rhône banks, and meander through the Old Town's winding lanes. Dutch painter Vincent Van Gogh also had a fondness for Arles, and it was here that he produced some of his most well-known pieces, such as **"Starry Night Over the Rhône"** and **"Café Terrace at Night."** With a self-guided walking tour of the artist's old haunts and preferred painting spots, tourists may now walk in Van Gogh's footsteps.

The Camargue: Situated to the west of Marseille, the Camargue is a huge natural park renowned for its distinct ecology, which includes wetlands, salt marshes, and lagoons. Black bulls, flamingos, and wild horses are among the many different species of plants and animals that call this pristine wilderness home.

Wandering about the park on foot, by bicycle, or on horseback allows visitors to enjoy the amazing landscape and see a variety of species. The Camargue is renowned for its historic ranches, where guests may experience the local cowboy way of life and see expert riders practice their riding and herding skills.

Villages of Luberon: The Luberon Villages are a **group of quaint, seemingly timeless hilltop towns and villages set within the undulating hills of the Luberon Regional Natural Park.** Every hamlet has its distinct personality and things to see and do, from the vibrant markets of L'Isle-sur-la-Sorgue to the charming alleys of Gordes. Explore antique churches and castles, meander down cobblestone lanes centuries old, and take in the relaxed ambiance of rural Provence. The Luberon Villages are the ideal location for a gourmet journey because of their excellent local food, which includes goat cheese, truffles, and superb wines.

In summary, there are many options for day trips and excursions from Marseille to Provence because of its fascinating history, breathtaking scenery, and lively culture. **This charming area of southern France has enough to offer everyone, whether you want to hike through unspoiled forests, see historic villages, or just relax on a quiet beach.** So gather your belongings, get on the road, and **be ready to be**

mesmerized by Provence's beauty and charm.

HISTORY AND CULTURE

Marseille is one of the oldest cities in France, with a vivid and rich history spanning over 2,600 years. Marseille has had a major influence on the history and culture of the Mediterranean area, from its modest origins as a Greek trade colony to its current position as a thriving cultural center.

A Synopsis of Marseille's:

Due to its advantageous position on the Mediterranean coast, Marseille, which was then known as Massalia, was founded around 600 BC by Greek sailors from Phocaea (modern-day Turkey). As a hub of trade and business, the city flourished, exchanging products with other Mediterranean civilizations including wine, olive oil, and ceramics.

Marseille was controlled by several different nations throughout the ages, including the Greeks, **Romans, Visigoths, and Franks, all of whom had an impact on the city's**

architecture and culture. Marseille rapidly became urbanized and industrialized throughout the 19th century, becoming a significant hub for trade and industry. Marseille is a vibrant, cosmopolitan city today that cherishes its rich past while gazing forward as a cutting-edge metropolis.

Architecture

Architecture: With a mix of medieval structures, ancient ruins, and contemporary constructions, Marseille's architecture is a reflection of its rich cultural past. Impacts of Rome and the Middle Ages:

Le Panier: Several of Marseille's oldest structures, including medieval churches, colorful homes, and winding cobblestone lanes, can be found in this ancient area. Built by Louis XIV in the 17th century, Fort **Saint-Jean is a magnificent example of military construction and provides sweeping views of the city and the ocean.** One of Marseille's most recognizable monuments is the majestic 19th-century Cathédrale La Major, which mixes Byzantine and Romanesque architectural elements. Contemporary and 19th-Century Developments.

La Cité Radieuse: La Cité Radieuse, a ground-breaking example of modernist architecture and a UNESCO World Heritage site, was created by renowned architect Le Corbusier.

Redevelopment of Vieux Port: Large-scale reconstruction efforts have been carried out in Marseille in recent years, and one such project was the revitalization of the Vieux Port neighborhood, which is now home to chic eateries, waterfront promenades, and contemporary structures.

Euroméditerranée: The goal of this large-scale urban regeneration project is to turn Marseille's port and waterfront region into a cutting-edge commercial center with high-tech residences, office buildings, and cultural attractions.

Literature and art: because of its rich history, breathtaking scenery, and lively culture, Marseille has long served as a creative haven for authors and artists.

Well-known Authors and Artists: The Dutch painter lived a large part of his life in Provence, which includes Marseille and the neighboring city of Arles. The natural beauty and light of the area served as inspiration for some of his most well-known paintings.

Marcel Pagnol: The well-known French writer and director was reared in Marseille and relied extensively on his early experiences there for his works of fiction and films, which often portrayed the common lives of Provence's working-class citizens.

Scene for Contemporary Art: Belle de Mai Friche: La Friche Belle de Mai is a vast cultural complex that houses a former tobacco factory and holds concerts, performances, and exhibits including modern theater, music, and art.

MUCEM: Situated on the waterfront, the Museum of European and Mediterranean Civilizations (MUCEM) is a stunning contemporary structure devoted to the study of the Mediterranean region's cultural legacy via anthropology, history, and art.

Customs and Traditions

Marseille has an abundance of customs and traditions, many of which have their roots in the city's past and rich cultural legacy.

Celebrations & Festivals: Fête de la Saint-Jean: Traditionally held on June 24th, this celebration of the summer solstice includes bonfires, music, and dancing in several areas across the city.

Marseille Jazz des Cinq Continents: Taking place in July, this annual jazz festival brings together leading local and international performers for a week of shows at various locations throughout Marseille.

Regional Folklore and Legends: The Legend of the Tarasque: Legend has it that a terrifying dragon-like monster known as the Tarasque once haunted Marseille. Saint Martha was able to tame the beast, and the town's residents finally killed it.

The Miracle of the Fishes: According to a different tale, Marseille was spared hunger during a famine thanks to a miraculous catch of fish in the Vieux Port. This story inspired the yearly custom of thanking the fishermen and their vessels.

In summary: history and culture span ancient Greece and Rome to contemporary France, creating a complex tapestry of influences that are as varied and dynamic as the city itself.

Marseille provides an enthralling window into the past, present, and future of the Mediterranean area, with its dynamic modern art scene, ancient ruins, and medieval architecture. **To grasp Marseille, take in the**

architectural marvels, dive into the thriving arts and cultural scene, and absorb the city's rich history.

FAMILY TRAVEL

With a plethora of sights and activities to suit all age groups, Marseille is an excellent family vacation location. This energetic Mediterranean city offers activities for all ages, including **kid-friendly workshops and courses, interactive museums, and outdoor experiences.**

Friendly Attractions for Families

Zoos and Aquariums: The Parc Zoologique de Marseille, located in the picturesque Parc Longchamp, is home to more than 130 different types of animals from all over the globe, including monkeys, giraffes, and elephants. With its roomy cages and informative displays, it's the ideal location for a fun family day.

Aquarium de Marseille: Situated in the Vieux Port, this underwater wonderland allows guests to investigate aquatic habitats from the Mediterranean Sea and other regions. This family-friendly attraction offers lots to see and learn about, from vibrant coral reefs to imposing sharks.

Parks & Playgrounds

Parc Borély: This expansive park on Marseille's outskirts has picnic spots, playgrounds, and acres of greenery, making it the ideal place for a family outing. Take a ride on a pedal boat rental on the lake, stroll around the botanical gardens, or just unwind in the sun.

Families love visiting the sandy beaches, water sports facilities, and shaded play spaces that the Parc Balnéaire du Prado, which is located along the Mediterranean coast, has to offer.

Kids' Workshop and Class Activities: Situated in the center of Marseille, Ateliers Kids provides kids aged three to twelve with a range of artistic workshops and programs. There is something for every child scientist or artist to enjoy, from food and scientific projects to arts and crafts and science experiments.

Musée des Civilisations de l'Europe et de la Méditerranée (MUCEM): Child-friendly museum Families will find MUCEM to be an excellent location because of its interactive displays and hands-on activities, even if it may not be geared exclusively for children. Children may explore the galleries and outdoor areas of the museum while learning about Mediterranean culture and history.

Advice for Taking Kids on VacationMake a Plan

To guarantee a seamless and joyful vacation for the whole family, plan and look into family-friendly lodging, activities, and food alternatives.

Pack Shrewdly: To keep the kids content and comfortable on your trip, pack food, water bottles, sunscreen, and entertainment for them.

Take pauses: Give yourself plenty of time to rest and unwind, particularly if you're taking little children on the trip. Schedule regular naps, playtime, and food periods to prevent tantrums and maintain a positive atmosphere for everybody.

Be Adaptable: Be open-minded and ready to modify your plans as necessary to take your family's needs and interests into account. When you accept unplanned excursions and go with the flow, you may sometimes make the finest memories.

Remain Safe: Whether you're enjoying outdoor activities or exploring the city's streets, don't forget to put safety first at all times. Observe your kids closely, particularly in busy or strange places, and make sure they know the fundamental safety precautions to take while traveling.

In summary: Marseille has a ton of family-friendly sights and things to do that will make your vacation one to remember. **This energetic Mediterranean city** has enough to offer everyone, whether you want to explore the city's cultural sites, go on outdoor activities, or just relax on the beach. **Prepare for an incredible journey in Marseille by packing your luggage, getting the family together, and getting ready!**

BUDGET ACCOMMODATIONS

Marseille is a vibrant city with plenty of options for travelers on a budget. From affordable accommodations to inexpensive dining and free activities, you can explore and enjoy Marseille without breaking the bank. **Here's a detailed guide to help you make the most of your trip while staying within your budget.**

Affordable Dining Options

Hostels: Vertigo Vieux-Port Hostel: Located just a short walk from the Old Port, this hostel offers dormitory and private rooms with modern amenities and a friendly atmosphere. Prices start at around €20 per night for a bed in a dorm.

The People Hostel: Situated near the train station, this hostel provides clean and comfortable accommodation with shared and private rooms. The communal areas are great for meeting other travelers. Rates start at approximately €22 per night for a dorm bed.

Budget Hotels

Hotel Hermès: This budget hotel in the Old Port area offers basic but clean and comfortable rooms, some with stunning views of the port. Rooms start at around €60 per night.

Ibis Budget Marseille Vieux Port: This chain hotel provides reliable and affordable lodging close to major attractions. Rooms are simple yet functional, with rates starting at €50 per night.

Vacation Rentals: Marseille has a variety of Airbnb options, from private rooms to entire apartments, often at very reasonable prices. Staying in an Airbnb can also allow you to cook some of your meals, saving on dining costs.

Affordable Dining Options

Street Food and Cafés: Le Marché des Capucins: This bustling market is a great place to sample local street food and pick up fresh produce. Try traditional Provençal dishes at budget-friendly prices.

Les Halles de la Major: A gourmet food market offering a variety of affordable dining options, from seafood to pastries. Enjoy your meal on the terrace with a view of the sea.

Budget Restaurants: Chez Étienne: Located in the Le Panier district, this popular pizzeria offers delicious wood-fired pizzas at reasonable prices. A pizza here typically costs around €10-€12.

Le Grain de Sable: This cozy café serves hearty and affordable meals, including salads, sandwiches, and daily specials. Expect to pay around €8-€12 for a meal.

Ethnic Eateries:

Taybeh: A small but vibrant Middle Eastern restaurant offering falafel, shawarma, and other delicious dishes at budget-friendly prices. Meals usually cost around €5-€10.

La Cantine de Nour: This North African eatery offers couscous, tagines, and other traditional dishes, with most meals priced under €15.

Free and Low-Cost Activities

Explore the Old Port: The Old Port (Vieux-Port) is the heart of Marseille and a great place to wander, people-watch, and enjoy the atmosphere. You can stroll along the waterfront, watch the boats, and enjoy the vibrant market.

Visit Basilique Notre-Dame de la Garde: This iconic basilica offers stunning views of the city and the Mediterranean Sea. Entry is free, and it's well worth the climb (or bus ride) up the hill for the panoramic views alone.

Wander Le Panier District: Le Panier is Marseille's oldest neighborhood, filled with narrow streets, colorful houses, and historic sites. It's free to explore and offers plenty of charming photo opportunities.

Relax at Parc Borély: This beautiful park is a perfect spot for a leisurely stroll, picnic, or paddleboat ride on the lake. The park is free to enter, and it's a great place to relax and enjoy nature.

Beach Day at Plage des Catalans: Located close to the city center, Plage des Catalans is a popular beach where you can swim, sunbathe, and play beach volleyball. It's free to access and a great spot for a budget-friendly day out.

MuCEM (Museum of European and Mediterranean Civilisations): While entry to the permanent exhibitions requires a ticket, the outdoor spaces and temporary exhibitions are often free. The museum's architecture and views alone make it worth a visit.

Money-Saving Tips

Use Public Transportation: Marseille's public transportation system is efficient and affordable. Purchase a 24-hour or 72-hour pass for unlimited travel on buses, trams, and the metro, which can save you money compared to single tickets.

Eat Like a Local: Avoid touristy restaurants and opt for local markets, bakeries, and small eateries where locals dine. You'll often find better prices and more authentic food.

Take Advantage of Free Days: Many museums in Marseille offer free entry on the first Sunday of each month. Plan your visits accordingly to save on admission fees.

Walk or Bike: Marseille is a walkable city, and exploring on foot is a great way to see the sights while saving money. Alternatively, consider renting a bike for a day to cover more ground affordably.

Book in Advance: For accommodations and attractions that require tickets, booking in advance can often secure lower prices. Look for online deals and discounts.

Travel Off-Peak: Visiting Marseille outside of the peak tourist season (June-August) can result in significant savings on flights, accommodations, and attractions. The weather is still pleasant in spring and fall, and there are fewer crowds.

Use Discount Cards: The Marseille City Pass offers free access to many museums, unlimited use of public transportation, and discounts on tours and activities. It's a great way to save if you plan on visiting multiple attractions.

In Summary: Marseille is an exciting and affordable destination for budget travelers. With a range of budget accommodations, inexpensive dining options, and plenty of free and low-cost activities, you can experience the best of what the city has to offer without spending a fortune. By following these money-saving tips, you'll be able to enjoy your trip to Marseille while keeping your expenses in check. **Happy travels!**

LGBTQ+ TRAVEL

Marseille is renowned for its active community, rich history, and varied culture, which includes a friendly environment for those who identify as LGBTQ+. Marseille, the second-biggest city in France, welcomes the LGBTQ+ community with a range of LGBTQ+-friendly spaces, pubs, nightlife, and events. **Marseille has a lot to offer, whether you're searching for a fun night out, cultural encounters, or simply a welcoming and safe atmosphere.**

LGBTQ+-Friendly Places

Le Cours JulienOne of Marseille's most creative and free-spirited districts is Cours Julien. It is well-known for its vibrant street art, hip cafés, and unique stores. The LGBTQ+ community also gathers here. Due to the abundance of LGBTQ+-friendly pubs and clubs in the region, both residents and visitors enjoy visiting it.

La Plaine: Located next to Cours Julien, this neighborhood also values individuality and inventiveness. It is often the hub of the alternative cultural scene in the city and is home to several LGBTQ+-friendly establishments. **It's a terrific spot to explore because of the vibrant environment and welcoming feel.**

Le Panier: One of Marseille's oldest and most beautiful neighborhoods, while not strictly an LGBTQ+ enclave. A mixed clientele is drawn to its attractive streets and old structures. The neighborhood is a lovely place for LGBTQ+ tourists to explore because of its artistic flare and friendly attitude.

Pubs and After-Dark

Activities

New Can-Can: One of Marseille's most well-liked LGBTQ+ pubs, New Can-Can is situated near the Cours Julien. With frequent themed evenings, drag acts, and DJ sets, it provides a vibrant environment. The pub is well-liked by both residents and tourists because of its welcoming atmosphere and personnel.

Le Pulse: Situated close to the Vieux Port, Le Pulse is an energetic nightclub. It has a large dance floor, an excellent sound system, and a range of musical selections, including pop and house. Regular LGBTQ+ activities at the club include drag shows and themed parties.

La Salle des Pas Perdus: Known for its welcoming and tolerant ambiance, this distinctive location combines elements of a pub and a cultural center. It's in the Le Panier neighborhood and holds a range of events, including parties that are LGBTQ+ friendly, art exhibits, and live music.

Le Got Milk? is a welcome LGBTQ+ pub with a laid-back vibe that is conveniently located in the center of Marseille. It's a fantastic spot to start the evening off or relax with friends over a beverage.

Events and Festivals

The major LGBTQ+ event in the city is Marseille Pride, commonly known as Marche des Fiertés. Every year in July, hundreds of people participate in and watch this colorful procession through Marseille's streets. In addition, there will be parties, concerts, and cultural events to support LGBTQ+ rights and visibility.

LGBT Film Festival: Every year, a wide range of movies that examine

LGBTQ+ topics and narratives are shown at Marseille's LGBT Film Festival. Festival programs include talks, screenings, and other activities that honor LGBTQ+ films and provide LGBTQ+ creators a stage. La Quinzaine des Fiertés is a two-week festival that celebrates LGBTQ+ culture and diversity. It takes place in advance of Marseille Pride. There is plenty for everyone in the community to do, with seminars, conferences, art displays, and parties among the activities.

Drag Shows and Performances: The drag culture in Marseille is flourishing, and regular shows are held at places like Le Pulse and New Can-Can. These events celebrate LGBTQ+ culture and provide high-energy entertainment with amazing drag performers from throughout the country and the world.

Resources for Safety and Assistance

General Advice on Safety: Remain Up to Date: Before you go, look for locations and activities that are LGBTQ+ friendly. Although Marseille is typically kind, you might feel safer and more at ease if you are prepared. Recognize Your Environment: Like in any big city, it's important to be mindful of your surroundings, particularly at night.

If at all possible, stay in well-lit locations and avoid wandering by yourself.

Honor regional traditions: Marseille is a welcoming city, but always be aware of and considerate of regional traditions. Resources for Assistance: Get in touch: This community-based LGBTQ+ group offers services and assistance. They provide health treatments, legal guidance, and counseling. Additional data and contact information may be found on their website, contact-groupe.org.

Le Refuge: Located in Marseille, Le Refuge is a national organization that provides support to young LGBTQ+ individuals who are homeless or have experienced rejection from their families. They offer social support, counseling, and short-term housing. Visit their website (le-refuge.org) for more details.

LGBTQI+ Center Marseille: This community center, which is situated in the city center, provides a secure environment for LGBTQ+ people. It offers resources on health, legal matters, and social support in addition to hosting events and workshops. For additional information, go to centre-lgbt-marseille.org.

AIDES: is a sexual health organization that offers services and support, including HIV testing and counseling. You can obtain free and private services at their branch in Marseille. They have more details on their website, aides.org.

In Summary: travelers who identify as LGBTQ+ can feel welcome in Marseille, a bustling, inclusive city. There's a lot to see, do, and experience, from vibrant nightlife and cultural festivals to helpful community resources. You can have a memorable and safe trip to this stunning Mediterranean city by exploring **LGBTQ+-friendly areas like Cours Julien and La Plaine, going to events like Marseille Pride, and making use of the available support services.**

SUSTAINABLE TRAVEL

Marseille is an excellent choice for eco-conscious travelers due to its breathtaking Mediterranean coastline and rich cultural legacy. The city has adopted environmentally friendly methods and provides visitors with a range of choices to reduce their impact on the environment. **Marseille offers a plethora of options for a conscientious and eco-friendly holiday, ranging from eco-friendly lodging and sustainable cuisine to volunteering and responsible tourism initiatives.**

Eco-Friendly Accommodation

Eco-Friendly Hotels: This downtown hotel has included several environmentally friendly practices, such as trash minimization plans, water conservation systems, and energy-efficient lighting. Visitors support sustainable practices while making use of contemporary conveniences.

NH Collection: Marseille The chain of NH Collection is renowned for its dedication to sustainability. Energy-efficient technologies, environmentally friendly toiletries, and a focus on waste reduction are all present at the Marseille site. Additionally, the hotel's central location makes it simple to use public transportation or stroll throughout the city.

Properties with Eco-Certification: Numerous hosts in Marseille provide eco-certified properties. Seek for listings that emphasize environmentally friendly practices, such as the use of natural cleaning supplies, recycling facilities, and energy-efficient equipment. Reducing your carbon impact may be facilitated by staying in an eco-certified apartment.

Greenly Preferred Hostels: Vertigo Hostel Vieux-Port: This hostel is an excellent choice if you're on a tight budget and want to focus on sustainability. It makes use of energy-saving lighting, supports recycling, and promotes eco-friendly and local excursions. Guests may experience sustainable city exploration because of the strategic location.

Farm-to-Table Restaurants that Promote Sustainability

Le Bistrot du Cours: This eatery, which is situated near Cours Julien, specializes in organic and locally sourced food. The menu is seasonal and varies to reflect what local farmers have to offer in terms of fresh products. Eating here cuts down on food miles and promotes sustainable agriculture.

Les Halles de la Major: Local and sustainable foods are given priority in many of the eating choices available at this gourmet food market. Savor locally produced goods like organic veggies, fresh seafood, and other delights while helping out your community.

Options for Vegetarians and Vegans: A menu brimming with vegetarian and vegan selections created with organic products is served at this café and restaurant. Their commitment to sustainability is shown by their support of fair trade goods and the use of biodegradable packaging.

Végét'Halles: Végét'Halles is a well-liked plant-based restaurant that serves a range of vegetarian and vegan options. To have as little negative influence on the environment as possible, the restaurant prioritizes utilizing organic and locally produced foods.

Zero-Waste Programs: This Marseille-based Italian eatery has embraced the zero-waste movement by putting into practice methods like composting food scraps, utilizing reused or biodegradable containers, and obtaining goods from nearby vendors that likewise use sustainable methods.

Conscientious Travel Approaches

Encourage regional companies: Select small, regional stores for your dining and shopping needs rather than big, worldwide corporations. In addition to boosting the regional economy, this lessens the carbon footprint left by long-distance freight transportation.

Limit Plastic Use: To cut down on single-use plastic waste, bring reusable shopping bags, cutlery, and water bottles. In Marseille, a lot of eateries and cafés are pleased to refill water bottles and value patrons who put sustainability first.

Eco-Friendly Transportation: Buses, trams, and metro are all part of Marseille's comprehensive public transit network. While visiting the city, using public transportation is a terrific method to lessen your carbon impact.

Walking and Biking: There are several bike rental choices, including electric cycles for those who want to cover more land, and the city is fairly walkable. Cycling in Marseille has become safer and simpler thanks to the city's growing network of bike lanes.

Save Water and Energy: Conscientious Use: Throughout your visit, be mindful of how much water and energy you use.

When not in use, turn off the lights, the air conditioner, and the heater. You may also save water by taking shorter showers.

Possibilities for VolunteeringEnvironmental Conservation: This group provides volunteer opportunities with an emphasis on community development and environmental conservation. Volunteers may take part in educational initiatives, marine conservation efforts, and reforestation. Visit their website **(planete-urgence.org)** for more details.

A group called Terre de Liens works to protect the Provence region's natural landscapes and advance sustainable agriculture. Volunteers may participate in educational initiatives that support sustainable practices as well as organic agricultural initiatives.

Community Service: Secours Catholique: This nonprofit offers a variety of volunteer options in Marseille, from helping in the community to taking part in social and educational initiatives for impoverished areas. For more information, go to secours-catholique.org, their website.

74

The Little Brothers of the Pauvres: With an emphasis on helping the elderly, this group invites volunteers to assist with social visits, event planning, and senior companionship. Visit their website, petitsfreresdespauvres.fr, for more details.

Cultural and Educational Programs: Community development initiatives, educational seminars, and cultural exchange programs are just a few of the volunteer options that France Volontaires provides in Marseille. Engaging in volunteer work with France Volontaires is an excellent method to contribute to the neighborhood while acquiring significant experience. **Further information is available on their website, France-Volontaires.org.**

In summary: in addition to being a stunning and culturally diverse city, Marseille supports sustainable travel methods. Travelers may experience a rewarding and ecologically responsible journey by selecting eco-friendly lodging, eating at sustainable restaurants, practicing responsible tourism, and volunteering. **Your sustainable decisions can help preserve Marseille's distinct appeal**

for future generations, whether you're exploring the lively districts, enjoying the regional food, or becoming involved in community initiatives.

HEALTH AND SAFETY

To guarantee a hassle-free and pleasurable vacation to Marseille, it's important to be well-informed about health and safety issues. Along with emergency services, the city provides a wide range of medical facilities, such as clinics, hospitals, and pharmacies. Knowing frequent scams and personal safety advice can give you confidence while navigating the city.

Medical Services

Marseille has some excellent medical facilities at its disposal. There are several solutions available, depending on whether you want emergency help or regular care.

Clinics and Hospitals: Hôpital de la Timone: Among Marseille's biggest and most esteemed medical facilities, Hôpital de la Timone provides a full range of medical services, including emergency care, specialist care, and cutting-edge technology. Situated at 264 Rue Saint-Pierre, it serves as the region's principal healthcare provider. Phone: (334) 91-38-00-00.

Hôpital Européen: This state-of-the-art hospital offers a comprehensive range of medical services, including orthopedic, oncological, and cardiac specialist treatments in addition to emergency care. The address is 6 Rue Désirée Clary. Phone: (334) 413-42-80-00..

Clinique Bouchard: A reputable private clinic that provides a range of medical services, including general medicine, surgery, and maternity care. The address is 77 Rue du Dr Escat. Phone: (334) 91-15-90 90.

Pharmacies

Marseille has a good distribution of pharmacies that sell a variety of prescription drugs and health-related items. For emergencies, many remain open late, and some even around the clock.

Pharmacie de la Joliette: With a large selection of goods and longer hours, this pharmacy is situated at 4 Place de la Joliette. Please call +33 4 91 90 71 62.

Pharmacie du Prado: Located at 10 Avenue du Prado, this pharmacy is renowned for its extensive assortment of health supplies and welcoming customer service. **Phone: (334) 91-53-00-90.**

Services and Numbers for Emergencies

Being aware of the following important numbers is essential in case of an emergency!

Emergency Services: 112 (European emergency number) (police, fire, ambulance).17. Fire Brigade (Pompiers): 18. Medical Emergencies (SAMU): 15. Local Police (Police Municipale): 17. These services provide prompt emergency response and are well-coordinated.

Staying Safe

Like any big metropolis, Marseille has some locations where one should exercise additional care. Keeping an eye on your surroundings and using common sense may greatly increase your safety.

Common Scams

Pick-pocketing: This is typical in tourist-heavy places like public transportation and Vieux Port. Keep your possessions safe and refrain from flaunting pricey objects. False charity:

Be wary of anyone who asks you for money to give to charity that seems questionable. It is advisable to turn them down gently and move on.

Exorbitant Taxis: Use authorized taxis or reliable ride-sharing services such as Uber at all times. To prevent getting overcharged, double-check the fare or make sure the meter is functioning.

Tips for Personal Safety

Preserve your well-lit areas: Stay on busy, well-lit streets at night. Steer clear of dimly lit or secluded locations, particularly if you are new to the region. Journey in Teams: Go with others whenever you can, especially after dark. When there are more people, there is safety.

Maintain Emergency Phone Numbers Practical: Make sure your phone is always loaded with the local emergency numbers. Carrying a card with these numbers on it is also a smart idea in case your phone is stolen or lost.

Handle Cash and Cards Carefully: Keep credit cards in a safe location and just carry the amount of cash you'll need for the day. Use ATMs that are situated in safe, well-lit areas—ideally, banks or large retail establishments.

Prevent Public Displays of Wealth: Steer clear of ostentatious jewelry and pricey accessories that might draw unwelcome attention. When not in use, keep cameras and other valuables hidden.

Make Reservations for Your Stay: Use the safe to store your belongings, and secure the doors and windows of your lodging at all times. Select lodgings with a decent security rating.

Remain Sober and Vigilant: Traveling is all about experiencing the local beverages, but always be mindful of your surroundings. Recognize your boundaries and never let your drink become unsupervised.

Understand Local Laws and Traditions: To prevent unintentionally upsetting people or causing difficulties, familiarize yourself with local laws and traditions.

Marseille is a bustling, stunning city with a lot to offer. By following these health and safety guidelines, you can make sure that your stay is both safe and pleasant. Being organized will help you get the most out of your vacation, whether you're taking part in its cultural activities, **dining in its delicious restaurants, or seeing its ancient areas.**

PRACTICAL INFORMATION

It is helpful to know the key contacts, local traditions, and navigational aids before visiting Marseille. You can make the most of your visit and traverse the city more skillfully with the aid of this useful information.

Local Customs and Etiquette

Marseille is a city rich in history and cultural variety. Gaining an understanding of regional traditions and social mores might improve your visit and facilitate more seamless interactions with residents.

Greetings: It's customary to shake hands when you first meet someone. **"La bise"** is customarily performed among friends and acquaintances, which is a quick kiss on both cheeks.

Title Use: Use titles such as **"Monsieur" (Mr.), "Madame" (Mrs.), or "Mademoiselle"**

(Miss) when addressing someone, particularly in formal settings. These titles should be followed by the person's last name.

Dining Etiquette: Table manners: Dining etiquette in France may be rather formal. Don't let your elbows cover your hands while they are on the table. When the host starts eating, wait to join them.

Bread: Instead of putting it on your main dish, place it immediately on the tablecloth or a separate plate.

Tipping: Although the bill often covers the cost of the service, it is traditional to offer a little tip (5–10%) if the service is satisfactory.

Clothing Code: Particularly when eating out or visiting sites, dress formally. In most situations, dress well yet casually; however, dress too casually for formal dining establishments or gatherings.

Useful Contacts and Resources

Public Conduct: When you go into stores or restaurants, always say "Bonjour" (good morning) or "Bonsoir" (good evening) to everybody. To be courteous, say "Merci" (thank you) and "S'il vous plaît" (please).

Silence: When in public, keep your voice quiet. Talking loudly is not acceptable, particularly while using public transportation. Beneficial Resources and Contacts Throughout your visit to Marseille, having a list of helpful contacts and resources might be very helpful. Law enforcement, firefighting, and ambulance services **(European Emergency Number: 112)** 17 local police officers **Emergency Medical Services (SAMU): 15;**

Tourist Information Centers

The Office de Tourisme et des Congrès de Marseille is situated at 11 La Canebière and provides information on local events and attractions as well as maps and brochures. Phone: **(33 4) 91-13-89-00.**

The Vieux Port Tourist Office is located close to the well-known Vieux Port and offers details on boat cruises, historical landmarks, and cultural events. Phone: (33 4) 91-13-99-50.

Consulates and Embassies

Marseille is home to several consulates that may provide a range of services, however, **the majority of embassies are situated in Paris.**

The US Consulate General is located at 15 Avenue Jules Cantini and may be reached at **+33 4 91 54 92 00**. The general consulates of the United Kingdom and Germany are located at 24 Avenue du Prado and 21 Rue des Catalans, respectively, and may be reached at **+33 4 91 15 72 10**. The hospital is located at 264 Rue Saint-Pierre and may be reached at **+33 4 91 38 00 00**.

6 Rue Désirée Clary; **+33 4 13 42 80 00**; Hôpital Européen.

Pharmacies: A green cross symbol is used in France to identify pharmacies. Many are open late, and others are open around the clock in case of need. The pharmacy located at 4 Place de la Joliette may be reached at +33 4 91 90 71 62.

Pharmacie du Prado: +33 4 91 53 00 90, 10 Avenue du Prado .Navigation and MapsMarseille's walkable city structure and well-developed public transportation system make navigating around the city very simple.

Maps and Navigation

Physical Maps: Marseille's major tourist destinations, public transportation lines, and walking trails are all highlighted on the free maps that are available at tourist information centers.

Online maps: For real-time navigation and locating sites of interest, Google Maps and other map applications are quite useful.

Public Transportation: Overseeing the bus, tram, and metro networks, RTM is Marseille's primary public transportation provider. They include maps, timetables, and ticket information on their website (rtm.fr).

Tickets and Passes: Tickets are available at kiosks, tram stops, and metro stations. Purchasing a day ticket or multiple-day pass may provide you with unrestricted access to RTM services.

Walking and Biking

A lot of Marseille's sights are accessible by foot, particularly in the city's core neighborhoods of Vieux Port, Le Panier, and La Canebière.

Bicycle Rentals: Le Vélo (levelo-mpm.fr) operates self-service bike stations, and Marseille offers other bike rental options. This is a practical and sustainable method of getting about the city.

Driving: Rental cars are available at the Marseille Provence Airport and other points throughout the city. In Marseille, big businesses like Europcar, Hertz, and Avis are present.

Parking: It might be difficult to find parking in the city center. Take public transportation into the city and park your car at public garages or park-and-ride lots outside. In brief

Your vacation experience will be improved by being aware of local traditions, having access to crucial contacts, and being able to explore Marseille with ease.

You may effortlessly blend into the lively culture of the city by adhering to local manners. Making use of the relevant resources—such as consulates and tourist information centers—guarantees that you will have assistance when you need it. Whether you're traveling by bike, foot, or public transportation, effective navigation enables you to confidently and easily explore Marseille. **You can fully appreciate all this stunning Mediterranean city has to offer if you prepare ahead of time.**

USEFUL PHRASES AND LANGUAGE GUIDE

Knowing a few simple phrases in French can help you have a much better trip to Marseille. Even though a lot of people, particularly in tourist regions, understand English, employing French expressions shows respect and may result in more pleasant encounters.

Basic French for Travelers

To assist you in overcoming the language barrier, this book offers helpful terminology, vocabulary, and resources.

Traveler's Basic French Gaining some basic French language skills can help you converse and feel more at ease while traveling. **The following are essential terms and expressions that any traveler has to use.**

Hi there (bohn-zhoor) - Salutations and good morning, **Bonsoir (bohn-swahr)** Greetings for the evening. Hi (informal) - Salut **(sah-loo)** Many thanks **(mehr-see) -** Regards If you will please excuse me **(seel voo**

), Please pardon me (ehk-skew-zay mwah). De Nul (Duh ree-ehn) - Thank you. Yes, we do. Sure.Not (oh).

Common Phrases

Sprechen Sie Englisch? Is your English language proficiency par-lay voo ahn-glay? My French is not very good. (zhuh nuh park pa bryan frahm-say) - My proficiency in French is lacking. Are you able to assist me? (poo-vay voo meh-day) – **Would you please aid me?** I am looking for... I'm trying to find (huh sheesh).

What is the cost of that? What is the price of (Kohm-been)?

Where is it? Oh my, **where is that?** Phrases Related to Travel:Je ... (voo-dray) - I'd want to...If it pleases you, the addition. (lah-dee-syon seel voo): Please, the bill.

Would you please have a table for two?

Please have a table for two (tah-bluh poor duh seel voo).

Where are the restrooms? Oh Sach Lay Twila-Let: Where are the bathrooms?Quelle est l'heure? Ah, kel - What time is it?

The appetizer (lahn-tree) - ArrivalThe exit (lah or-tee) - Go out of Gare () - Station for trains

Frequently Used Expressions Not only may understanding these popular terms help you converse more naturally with locals, but it can also help you better comprehend their reactions. Is it combined with dining out? Say **"kohm-been"** and ask how much it is. Please reserve a table for me. (huh voo-dray ray-zayr-vary soon Utah-blue) – I want to make a table reservation. Please have a glass of wine. A glass of wine, please (uh duh van seel voo pleh).La carte, if . **(please, please, please)** - The menu. It is delicious! Say **"day-lee-syuh"**; it's that tasty!

Directions and Mode of Transportation: Where is the area located? Oo eh lah -

What is the location of the train station? I want to purchase a ticket. **(huh voo-dray ah-shay-tay un bee-yay)** – I want to purchase a pass. Is it far away? Saying **"lawn"** : **Is it far?** Turn to the left. (toor-nay ah gosh): Make a left turn. Make a right turn. (toor-nay ah): Make a right turn.

Modifications: Do you have a spare room available? Yes, please have a room available **(ah-vay voo on shahm-bruh lee-bruh). For what many nights?** How many nights, **oh**

pitiful kohm-been duh ? I would like to book a room. To book a room, say (voo-dray ray-zayr-vay shahm-bruh). What time does the petit-déjeuner start? (ah kel eh puh-tee day-zhuh-nay) - What time is breakfast?

Resources and Apps for Language Learning

Some very helpful applications and tools are available for tourists who want to learn more French or who require instant access to translations.

Applications for Learning Languages: With Duolingo: Fun and simple-to-follow bite-sized lessons are provided by this well-known software. It works well for learning vocabulary and simple sentences.

Babbel: Babbel offers interactive conversations with an emphasis on conversational skills to help you practice speaking French.Rosetta Stone: renowned for its immersive methodology, Rosetta Stone facilitates learning via visual clues and context, which helps you remember what you learn.

Apps for translation: Google Translate: This program provides real-time text, speech, and even picture translation. For on-the-go, rapid translations, it's invaluable. Microsoft

Translation This program has speech and text translation capabilities, as well as a phrasebook function for frequently used terms, much like Google Translate.i

Translate: This program enables back-and-forth language communication in a conversation style while offering text and voice translation.Internet-based sources: French beginner classes and free resources, including audio and video materials, are provided by BBC Languages.

FrenchPod101: Offers word lists, study aids, and a range of audio and video classes. For tourists who want to become better at speaking and listening, it's a great resource. Linguee: An excellent online dictionary that explains words and phrases in context by providing translations and sample sentences.

Lonely Planet phrasebooks Dictionary & Phrasebook in French: A handy pocket or purse size reference that is both thorough and small. For easy reference, it's ideal.

The Rick Steves French Phrase Book & Dictionary is an excellent additional resource that offers cultural advice and useful terms to improve your trip.

You'll be in a better position to interact with people and fully experience Marseille culture if you pick up a little basic French and make use of these tools.

Your attempts to speak French will be valued and will enhance your trip experience whether you're placing an order, getting directions, or interacting with people.

DIRECTORY

Possessing an extensive directory at your disposal may greatly enhance the convenience and pleasure of your stay in Marseille. Comprehensive lists for lodging, dining establishments, tour companies, conveyance services, and emergency contacts are provided below. **You may plan your vacation, make bookings, and deal with any unanticipated circumstances with the aid of these services.**

Listings for Accommodations

Marseille has a variety of lodging choices to fit every taste and budget. **The following suggestions are divided into many categories.**

Luxury Hotels: The InterContinental Marseille - Hotel Dieu is housed in a landmark structure with opulent facilities, breathtaking vistas, and a fine dining establishment. **1 Place Daviel, 13002 Marseille is the address. Telephone: (334) 1342-4242.**

The Sofitel Marseille Vieux-Port: This hotel, which is close to the Vieux Port, offers luxurious accommodations, a spa, and top-notch eating choices. 36 Boulevard Charles Livon, 13007 Marseille is the address. Call: (334) 91-15-59-00.

Boutique Hotels: Hôtel C2: A stylish 19th-century home turned boutique hotel with a tranquil spa and modern furnishings. 48 Rue Roux de Brignoles, 13006 Marseille is the address. Phone number: (334) 95-05-13.

The chic and contemporary Alex Hotel & Spa is close to the Saint-Charles train station and has cozy accommodations in addition to a spa. 13–15 Place des Marseillaises, 13001 Marseille is the address. Telephone: (333) 413-24-13-24.

Mid-Range Hotels: Hotel Carré Vieux Port: Perfect for touring the city, this centrally situated hotel offers cozy accommodations and kind service. 6 Rue Beauvau, 13001

Marseille is the address. **Telephone: (334) 91–33–66–97.** Oceania Marseille Escale Vieux Port: Provides a superb location, contemporary facilities, and a comfortable and convenient combination. 5 La Canebière, 13001 Marseille is the address. Telephone: **(334) 91-99-23 23.**

Low-cost Hotels & Hostels: Vertigo Vieux-Port is a well-known hostel with a great location, a sociable vibe, and both private and dorm accommodations. 38 Rue Fort Notre Dame, 13007 Marseille is the address. **Phone number (334) 9164-42-95.** Première Classe Hotel Marseille Center: Comfortable and reasonably priced, conveniently located near main attractions. 13 Rue Lafon, 13006 Marseille is the address. Call: (33 4) 91-92-00-20.

Vacation Rentals and Apartments: There are many Airbnb listings in Marseille, ranging from opulent mansions to affordable flats. For the greatest experience, look for real estate in areas like Vieux Port, Le Panier, and La Corniche. Marseille Center Staycity Aparthotels Fully furnished apartments with hotel-quality facilities are available in Vieux Port. 11 Rue de Ruffi, 13002 Marseille is the address. **Call: (33 4) 91-37-82-20.**

Restaurant Listings

The food scene in Marseille is lively and varied, with everything from fancy restaurants to family-friendly cafés. Here are a few noteworthy choices:

Fine Dining: Le Petit Nice Passedat: a Michelin-starred restaurant renowned for its mouthwatering Mediterranean fare and shellfish. Address: 13007 Marseille, Anse de Maldormé - Corniche J.F. Kennedy. **Tel: (33 4) 91-59-25-92.**

Entre Table, au Sud: inventive cooking accompanied with breathtaking views of the Vieux Port. 2 Quai du Port, 13002 Marseille is the address. Phone: (334) 91-90-63-53.

Mid-Range Options: Chez Fonfon: Known for its bouillabaisse, this eatery provides genuine Provençal cuisine in a quaint atmosphere. 140 Rue du Vallon des Auffes, 13007 Marseille is the address. Caller number: +33 4 91 52 14 38. L'Épuisette: a seafood-focused restaurant with elegant cuisine and stunning views. Vallon des Auffes, 13007 Marseille is the address. **Call: (33 4) 91-52-17-82.**

Cheap Eats: Le Café des Épices: a welcoming café with reasonably priced, tasty, and fresh food. 4 Rue du Lacydon, 13002 Marseille is the address. Call: (33 4) 91-91-22-69.Au Falafel: A Mediterranean snack and a fast and tasty falafel sandwich option. 15 Rue de Lodi, 13006 Marseille is the address. **Call: (33 6) 28-51-19 71.**

Bakeries and cafés: La Samaritaine: A charming patio overlooking the Vieux Port, this historic café is the ideal place for light fare or coffee. 2 Quai du Port, 13002 Marseille is the address. **Phone number (33 4): 90 36 64 91.**

Bakery Sylvain Depuichaffray: Well-known for its cakes, pastries, and confections. 66 Rue Grignan, 13001 Marseille is the address. **Telephone: (33 4) 91-54-91.**

Nightlife and Bars: Le Carry Nation is a speakeasy bar with a mood reminiscent of the Prohibition period and masterfully made drinks.

Address: Hidden location; online reservations only. Classic Bar Bar de la Marine has a lively atmosphere and fantastic views of the Vieux Port. 15 Quai de Rive Neuve, 13001 Marseille is the address. **Tel: (33 4) 91-54-95 42.** Travel Agencies Taking a guided tour of Marseille might provide more in-depth knowledge and distinctive encounters. Here are a few trustworthy tour companies:

Tour Operators

Marseille Walking Tours: Provides guided walking tours that encompass cultural monuments, historical locations, and undiscovered attractions. **Call +33 6 51 21 06 18 or visit marseillewalkingtours.com to book a tour.**

Le Vélo Touristique: This trip blends walking and bicycling to discover the city's many facets. Levelotouristique.com; +33 4 91 59 44 95; phone.

Tours by Boat: Croisières Marseille Calanques: Focuses on providing boat trips to the Calanques, Château d'If, and other sights along the coast. Phone: +33 4 91 33 66 55; **website:** croisières-marseille-calanques.com.Icard Maritime: Provides a range of boat excursions, such as private charters and sunset cruises. **Phone: +33 4 91 13 89 00;**

Discover Provence: Provides personalized excursions with an emphasis on the history, food, and culture of the area. **Phone: +33 4 91 33 66 33;**

website: discover-provence.net.Services for

TransportationMarseille's extensive transit network makes getting about the city simple. The following are some essential services:

Transportation Services

Public Transportation: The Marseille bus, tram, and metro systems are run by the RTM (Régie des Transports Métropolitains). Telephone: **+33 4 91 91 92 10.**

Website: Offers national and regional rail services, including TGV trains that travel at high speeds. SNCF website; **phone: +33 8 92 35 35 35**. Hertz offers car rentals at the Marseille Provence Airport and several city sites. The website is hertz.com. Telephone: (33 4) 91-50-53.Avis: Provides a large selection of cars for hire across the city. Via **phone: +33 4 91 50 50 00**; website: avis.com.Services for

Taxis: Dependable cab service available throughout the city. Phone number: 03-34-01-02-20.Allo Taxi: Another well-known taxi service that operates around the clock. Caller ID: **+33 4 91 92 92**.

Carpooling: A popular option for easy and adaptable transportation in Marseille. Uber.com is a website.

Contacts for Emergencies

For your safety and peace of mind, it's crucial to know the main emergency contacts while traveling in Marseille. Emergency Services in General: For police, fire, and medical emergencies, dial 112 in Europe.

Hospitals and Clinics: Full medical treatment, including after-hours assistance. 264 Rue Saint-Pierre, 13005 Marseille is the address. Telephone: (33) 491-38-00

BUSINESS AND CONFERENCES

Marseille, a bustling port city in southern France, is becoming a more important convention and business center in addition to being a well-liked vacation spot. It **is the perfect place to organize corporate gatherings because of its advantageous position on the Mediterranean coast, good transportation connections, and variety of amenities.** Marseille has lots to offer, regardless of whether you're attending a conference, organizing a business trip, or looking for networking chances.

Conference Centers

Marseille is home to several cutting-edge conference facilities that can accommodate gatherings of all shapes and sizes.

Here are a few of the best locations

Parc Chanot - Situated in the center of the city, Parc Chanot is one of the best locations for exhibits and conferences. It has several halls and conference spaces that can hold up to 7,000 people. The facility **offers expert support services, Wi-Fi, and state-of-the-art audiovisual equipment to guarantee the success of any event.** Rond-Point du Prado, 13008 Marseille is the address. Call: (33 4) 91-76-1600. Parc-chanot.com is the website.

World Trade Center Marseille Provence: Located in the heart of the city, the World Trade Center provides a variety of conference spaces and meeting rooms that are ideal for business purposes. It has video conferencing capabilities, fast internet, and on-site technical assistance. Workshops, business meetings, and smaller conferences are ideal at this location.

Address: 13001 Marseille, 2 Rue Henri Barbusse. Phone number:

0334-13-94-20-00. wtcmp.com is a website.

Palais du Pharo: With its breathtaking views of the Mediterranean and Old Port, the ancient Palais du Pharo offers a sophisticated venue for business gatherings. It has an auditorium that can hold up to **900 people and other meeting rooms.** The location is a distinctive option for any occasion since it blends contemporary conveniences with historic charm. **Phone: +33 4 91 14 64 95**; address: 58 Boulevard Charles Livon, 13007 Marseille. Marseille-tourisme.com is the website.

Docks des Suds: Docks des Suds provides a flexible location that may be tailored for a range of events, including business conferences, trade exhibitions, and cultural events if you're looking for a less traditional setting. The facility, which has an industrial vibe, is well-known for its vast open areas and lively atmosphere. Tel: +33 4 91 99 00 00; Address: 12 Rue Urbain V, 13002 Marseille. Dock-des-suds.org is the website.

Business-Friendly Hotels

Many hotels in Marseille are designed with business travelers in mind, offering a variety of facilities and services to make your stay efficient.

Here are a few highly suggested items

Hotel Dieu - InterContinental Marseille: For business visitors, this opulent hotel has excellent amenities including a business center, high-speed internet, and well-equipped conference rooms. It is an easy option for getting to important commercial sectors because of its strategic position close to the Vieux Port.

Phone: +33 4 13 42 42 42; address: 1 Place Daviel, 13002 Marseille; website: ihg.com.

The Sofitel Marseille Vieux-Port: Offering a conference center, meeting rooms, and a fully furnished business center, Sofitel is a luxurious hotel with breathtaking views of the Old Port. The hotel is a great starting point for business visitors because of its opulent suites and top-notch dining choices.

Phone: +33 4 91 15 59 00; Address: 36 Boulevard Charles Livon, 13007 Marseille. Sofitel.accor.com is the website.

Marseille's Radisson Blu Hotel Vieux Port: The Radisson Blu, which is situated in the core of the city, has contemporary conference spaces, fast internet, and a 24-hour business center. The hotel is well-liked by business visitors due to its outstanding facilities and handy location. 38–40 Quai de Rive Neuve, 13007 Marseille is the address. **Telephone: (334) 488-44-52-52.**

Radissonhotels.com is the website.

The Novotel Marseille Port Vieux: The Novotel is a dependable option for business visitors as it provides a business center, conference space, and roomy accommodations. It is a sensible choice for business stays due to its proximity to the Old Port and important commercial districts. 36 Boulevard Charles Livon, 13007 Marseille is the address.

Call: (334) 961-11-42 11. Novotel.accor.com is the website.

Opportunities for Networking

Marseille's thriving business community and regular events provide plenty of chances for networking and professional growth. The following are some strategies to build your network and get in touch with other professionals:

Chambers of Commerce: The Chamber of Commerce and Industry (CCI) in Marseille Provence For both domestic and foreign firms, the CCI hosts a variety of events, training, and networking opportunities. You may grow your business network and make connections with important industry leaders by attending these events. The address is 9 La Canebière, Palais de la Bourse, 13001 Marseille. **Phone number: (33 4) 91-39-34.** ccimp.com is a website.

Conferences and Business Events: Euroméditerranée: Often hosting corporate and urban development-oriented conferences, seminars, and networking events, Euroméditerranée is one of the biggest urban redevelopment initiatives in Europe. By going to these gatherings, one may make insightful contacts. Euromediterranee.fr is the we website.

Professional Associations: Provence's French-American **Chamber of Commerce (FACC):** This organization hosts monthly business luncheons, networking nights, and seminars. These are great occasions to network with industry peers and learn about potential commercial ventures between France and the US. Faccnyc.org is the website.

Co-working Spaces: Le Loft Coworking Marseille provides

entrepreneurs, freelancers, and business travelers with a collaborative atmosphere. To encourage members to interact and work together, frequent social gatherings, seminars, and networking events are planned. 35 Rue Sainte, **13001 Marseille is the address. Telephone: (33 4) 91-91-91-91. Leloft Marseille's website.**

Coworking Marseille: Another well-liked co-working facility that offers adaptable office space and organizes gatherings to promote networking and company growth. 3 Place Félix Baret, 13006 Marseille is the address.

Telephone: (33 4) 91-58-55-67. CoworkinMarseille.fr is the website.

Industry-Specific Meetups: Marseille Innovation: This incubator and accelerator gives companies and innovators from a range of sectors monthly events, pitch sessions, and networking opportunities. By taking part in these events, you may network with possible investors and partners and remain up to date on industry trends, Marseille-innovation.com is the website.

In summary: with its cutting-edge conference centers, business-friendly lodging options, and plenty of networking possibilities, **Marseille is**

a bustling city that welcomes business visitors.

Marseille offers a helping and motivating atmosphere for business operations, whether you are organizing company meetings, attending a conference, or trying to grow your professional network. Combining work with pleasure in Marseille is both sensible and pleasurable, **thanks to its dynamic metropolitan life, breathtaking seaside vistas, and rich cultural legacy.**

SPECIAL INTEREST TRAVEL

For those who want to go deeper into really unique experiences, **Marseille has a variety of special interest travel alternatives thanks to its varied geography and rich cultural past.** Every tourist will find something to enthrall them in Marseille and its environs, regardless of their interests in wine, health, or adventure.

Wine Tours and Visits to Vineyards

Marseille and the surrounding area of Provence are known **for their excellent wines, especially rosé.**

Savoring fine wines and taking in the stunning Provençal landscape may be had by visiting nearby wineries.

Château La Coste: An hour's drive from Marseille, Château La Coste is a destination for art and architecture in addition to being a vineyard. Wine tastings, vineyard tours with a guide, and modern art pieces dotted across the property are available to visitors. It's a one-of-a-kind experience, enhanced by the pairing of exquisite wine and contemporary art.

Address: 13610 Le Puy-Sainte-Réparade, 2750 Route de La Cride. Tel: (334) 42-61-92-90. Chateau-la-coste.com is the website.

Domaine Tempier: Offering tastings and guided tours, Domaine Tempier is located in the Bandol area, which is well-known for its bold red wines and sophisticated rosés. The estate, which has been in the family since 1834, has a long and illustrious past. Walking through the vineyards, seeing the cellars, and tasting their renowned wines are all included in a visit here.

The address is 83330 Le Plan du Castellet, Route des Mourvèdres. Tel: (33 4) 94-98-70 70. Domaine-Tempier.com is the website.

Château de Calavon: With its organic wines, Château de Calavon, located in the center of the Aix-en-Provence wine area, provides a lovely experience. Visitors may take a tour of the vineyards, see how wine is made, and partake in tastings in a quaint environment. 10 Boulevard Léonce Artaud, **13680 Lançon-Provence is the address. Call: (334) 42-87-02-79.** the calavon.com website.

Spa and Wellness Getaways

Marseille offers several spa and health facilities where guests may relax and renew in stunning surroundings. These resorts provide a genuinely healing experience by combining holistic health techniques with luxury.

The InterContinental Marseille: Cinq Mondes Spa, housed in a landmark structure with breathtaking views of the Old Port, provides a selection of treatments influenced by international customs. The spa guarantees a full health experience, with treatments ranging from Balinese massages to Japanese baths. 1 Place Daviel, 13002 Marseille is the address. Telephone: (334) 1342-43. ihg.com is a website.

Spa Sofitel Marseille Vieux-Port: This opulent spa provides a range of rejuvenating and relaxing treatments. The spa offers a variety of massages and cosmetic treatments, a sauna, a hammam, and a stunning view of the Old Port. 36 Boulevard Charles Livon, **13007 Marseille is the address. Call: (33 4) 91-15-59-97. Sofitel.accor.com is the website.**

Carita Spa at Hôtel C2: Tucked away in a stately home, Spa Carita offers a serene environment for spa services. Using Carita's well-known skincare products, the spa provides customized treatments that guarantee a sumptuous and productive experience. 48 Rue Roux de Brignoles, **13006 Marseille is the address. Website: hotel-c2.com; phone: +33 4 95 05 13 13.**

Adventure Tourism

Marseille and the neighboring areas provide a multitude of thrilling activities for adventure seekers that take full use of the region's varied natural surroundings.

Rafting and Canyoning

One of the best places to go rafting and canyoning is the Verdon Gorge, which is around two hours drive from Marseille. These activities are set against the exhilarating background of the Verdon River's gorgeous blue waters. Different tour providers provide guided tours with varying degrees of expertise. Both novice and expert explorers may enjoy the rafting and canyoning tours offered by Aqua Viva Est. Their knowledgeable guides guarantee an exciting and risk-free experience. **Phone: +33 4 92 77 73 67; Address: Route de Castellane, 04120 La Palud-sur-Verdon. Surf over to aquaviva-est.com.**

Caving and Exploration

The intriguing cave systems of Marseille are ideal for exploration thanks to the region's distinctive limestone geology. Spelunking, also known as caving, is an exciting way to explore the area's underground treasures.

Expé Nature: Offers guided cave tours in the Calanques and neighboring regions. These tours provide a distinctive viewpoint of the area's natural beauty as they explore stunning caves and underground rivers. Phone: +33 6 68 88 96 56; Address: 8 Chemin du Littoral, 13008 Marseille; website: expe-nature.com.

In summary: Marseille offers a diverse array of special interest travel alternatives to fit a broad variety of interests and passions, guaranteeing that each tourist will discover an experience that speaks to them. Marseille has something for everyone, whether they are seeking the excitement of outdoor experiences, indulging in opulent spa treatments, or tasting the best wines. **Take advantage of everything that this dynamic city and its environs have to offer to craft unique experiences catered to your interests.**

MARSEILLE ON A BUDGET

You may enjoy Marseille, a city renowned for its lively culture and rich history, without going over budget. You may travel economically to this stunning Mediterranean location if you plan carefully. **Here are some suggestions and advice for visiting Marseille on a tight budget, with an emphasis on free or inexpensive activities, reasonably priced restaurants, and lodging options.**

Low-Cost and Free Attractions

The Vieux Port, also known as the Old Port, is a busy place in the center of Marseille where you can promenade, observe the boats, and take in the ambiance all for free. Enjoying street performances and local markets is another wonderful thing to do in the ancient port area. **Discover Marseille's oldest district, Le Panier District, with its charming tiny lanes, vibrant residences, and creative atmosphere.**

Le Panier is completely free to explore and seems like a step back in time. Take note of the street art and murals that cover a lot of the walls.

Basilique Notre-Dame de la Garde: Although admission to this magnificent church is free, the high position of the basilica affords incomparable panoramic views of Marseille. With its striking views of the metropolis and the Mediterranean Sea, the basilica is a well-known emblem of the city. **The magnificent architecture of the Museum of European and Mediterranean Civilizations (MuCEM) and its outdoor spaces, such as the J4 Esplanade and Fort Saint-Jean, are free to explore, while admission to the major displays is charged.** These areas provide beautiful picnic spots with amazing views.

Palais Longchamp: The Museum of Fine Arts and the Natural History Museum are housed in this opulent

19th-century edifice, although the entrance is free to enjoy the gardens and fountains on the property. The nearby park is ideal for a leisurely walk. A beautiful public park, Parc Borély has a lake, well-designed gardens, and plenty of open areas for lounging and picnics. It's free to relax and take in the scenery at Parc Borély.

National Park of Calanques: While trekking through the breathtaking Calanques is free, there may be fees associated with certain park activities. The hikes provide breathtaking views of the rocky shoreline and azure ocean. You just need to bring water and some snacks for an amazing day of exploration.

Affordable Eateries

La Boîte à Sardine, well-known for its **fresh fish**, serves reasonably priced meals that highlight Marseille's characteristics. It's a beloved spot in the community where you can eat well without going over budget. **Address: 13001 Marseille, 2 Boulevard de la Libération. Telephone: (334) 91-50-95-95.**

Le Panier à Burgers: This laid-back restaurant in the Le Panier neighborhood offers expensive but delicious gourmet burgers. It's a terrific place to have a filling lunch while exploring the neighborhood. 10 Rue des Petits Puits, 13002 Marseille is the address. Phone number: 03-34-091-31-51.

Avec Etienne: A landmark in the community, Chez Etienne is well-known for its wood-fired pizzas and straightforward yet delectable Mediterranean fare. Because of the affordable pricing, both residents and tourists like going there. 43 Rue Lorette, 13002 Marseille is the address. Phone number (334) 491-54-76-33.

Chez Noël: Authentic Provencal food is served in this classic café at reasonably priced pricing. The cuisine offers regional specialties like ratatouille and aioli, giving visitors a true experience of Marseille. 23 Rue d'Izoard, 13001 Marseille is the address. Call: (334) 91-48-92-09.

Marché des Capucins: Sample a range of street delicacies and fresh vegetables at the Marché des Capucins for an inexpensive supper. The market is a bustling spot to get a quick snack and learn about the regional cuisine.

Budget-Friendly Accommodation

Vertigo Vieux-Port Hostel: This hostel, which is located near the Old

Port, has reasonably priced individual and dorm accommodations. Its convenient location and welcoming environment make it a popular option for low-cost vacationers. 38 Rue Fort Notre Dame, 13007 Marseille is the address. Phone number **(334) 9164-42-95.** hostel-marseille.fr is the website.

Hotel Terminus Saint-Charles: This hotel offers cozy accommodations at reasonable rates close to the Saint-Charles rail station. For individuals who are coming by train and want simple access to public transit, it's a practical choice. Phone: +33 4 91 90 74 95; Address: 1 Place des Marseillaises, 13001 Marseille. Hotel-terminus-saint-charles.fr is the website.

The inexpensive Hotel Première Classe Marseille Centre is conveniently situated and has basic but cozy accommodations. It's a great starting point for seeing the city without going over budget for lodging. +33 4 91 92 82 25.

Address: 13 Rue Lafon, 13006 Marseille. PremiereClasse.com is the website.

Vacation rentals and Airbnb: If you're looking for something more like a home for a longer stay, try renting a vacation house or using Airbnb. Private rooms and whole apartments are available, sometimes at a lesser cost than at conventional hotels. This might be especially economical for larger families or gatherings.

The Jeunesse Auberge de Bois Luzy: Situated in a stunning house from the 19th century, this youth hostel is a short distance from the city center. In addition to a tranquil garden, it provides extremely affordable individual rooms and dorm accommodations. 58 Allée des Primevères, 13012 Marseille is the address. Contact: +33 4 91 45 27 64. hi-france.org is the website.

In summary: Marseille may be visited and enjoyed without breaking the bank because of its beautiful scenery, rich cultural history, and energetic local community. You may enjoy the finest of this Mediterranean jewel without breaking the bank by making use of free activities, dining at reasonably priced restaurants, and booking reasonably priced lodging.

 Enjoy Marseille and everything that this lovely city has to offer, including its distinct charm and kind welcome. Updates and Expectations in Marseille for 2024

The second-largest city in France and a historically significant port, Marseille, is constantly changing as a result of a fusion of contemporary growth and cultural legacy. Several fascinating developments and activities are anticipated in 2024 to increase the city's allure for both residents and tourists. This is a comprehensive look at what to anticipate in Marseille in 2024, from cultural events to infrastructural upgrades.

Urban Development and Infrastructure

Euromediterranee Project: One of Europe's biggest urban regeneration projects, the continuing Euroméditerranée project, is expected to advance significantly in 2024.

Through the establishment of additional residential, commercial, and recreational spaces, this initiative seeks to rejuvenate the shoreline and its environs. Viewers may anticipate contemporary architecture, landscaped areas, and enhanced public amenities. Adding more tramway service via this area will improve connection even further.

Expansion of Marseille-Provence Airport: To accommodate growing passenger volumes and enhance the overall experience, Marseille-Provence Airport is undertaking major renovations. The airport is anticipated to open a larger terminal by 2024 with improved facilities, expedited security checks, and more places to eat and shop. This will facilitate and improve the pleasure of traveling to and from Marseille.

Green spaces and ecodistricts: Marseille is dedicated to environmentally friendly urban development. There are now many new eco-districts under construction that will include public parks, green roofs, and energy-efficient structures. With an emphasis on lowering carbon footprints, initiatives like the "Smartsville" ecodistrict seek to provide a sustainable living environment. These programs will increase the city's attractiveness to tourists who care about the environment.

Highlights of Culture and Events Summer Olympics in 2024

Sailing Events With the sailing contests coming to Marseille in 2024, the city will be a major player in the Summer Olympics. The waterfront and port parts of the city have been ready to receive athletes and spectators.

Marseille's potential as a premier sports destination will be highlighted by this important tournament, which will draw attention from across the world. Anticipate lively activities in the vicinity of the Vieux Port and the shore, in addition to a range of associated cultural events and celebrations.

Festival d'Aix-en-Provence: Despite taking place in the adjacent town of Aix-en-Provence, this well-known opera festival will continue to bring tourists to the area. The festival is anticipated to have an incredible roster of acts in 2024, drawing opera enthusiasts from all over the globe. For those staying in the city, the cultural excursion is easily accessible due to its closeness to Marseille.

Cultural Exhibitions with MuCEM: In 2024, the Museum of European and Mediterranean Civilizations (MuCEM) is expected to remain a prominent cultural center, hosting several prestigious exhibits. **These exhibits will look at a range of historical, cultural, and modern topics related to the Mediterranean region.** Anticipate captivating exhibitions, interactive displays, and educational events that deepen visitors' comprehension of the area.

Marseille Jazz des Cinq Continents: In 2024, this yearly jazz festival is expected to provide an even more remarkable and varied program. The event, which will take place at several locations across the city, **including the magnificent Palais Longchamp, will include both local and international jazz musicians.** For fans of music, it's an event not to be missed, providing an opportunity to see elite acts in stunning venues.

Renovations and New Attractions
Le Corbusier's building, La Cité Radieuse

 Often referred to as the **"Radiant City,"** La Cité Radieuse is among Le Corbusier's most well-known architectural creations. **Renovations to improve the tourist experience are scheduled for 2024, and one of the anticipated improvements is better access to the rooftop terrace, which offers breathtaking views of the city and the Mediterranean.** The structure is a major draw for those who love architecture since it includes a museum, a hotel, and other cultural venues.

Vallon des Auffes: This charming fishing harbor is being renovated to strengthen its infrastructure while maintaining its historic character. It is located close to the city center. Better pedestrian access, more food options, and renovated amenities will make the area even more enjoyable for tourists to explore by 2024.

Parc National des Calanques expansion: It is anticipated that tourist amenities and conservation initiatives will be strengthened in the Calanques National Park, which is well-known for its striking limestone cliffs and blue seas. Better trash management methods, hiking pathways, and educational signs will all contribute to the preservation of this natural jewel while also improving accessibility and enjoyment for outdoor lovers.

Improvements in Transportation
Extensions of the Tramway and Metro

To accommodate the city's burgeoning population and tourism, Marseille's public transportation system is developing. **Better connectivity will be available across the city in 2024 with the completion of new tramway lines and metro expansions.** Travelers will find it simpler to go between the airport, neighborhoods, and main attractions as a result.

Bike-sharing and Eco-Mobility: Marseille is expanding its bike-sharing program and creating additional bike lanes all across the city to encourage environmentally friendly transport. There will be new electric scooters and bike rental stations to encourage visitors and locals alike to explore the city in an environmentally friendly manner. The ultimate goal of this project is to improve urban living conditions and lessen transportation congestion.

Dining and Hospitality

New lodging options: In 2024, several new hotels are expected to debut, giving travelers additional choices. There are several options to fit a range of preferences and price ranges, from boutique hotels housed in historic structures to contemporary, environmentally friendly lodgings. Marseille's hospitality scene will be improved by these new businesses, which will provide first-rate facilities and services.

Culinary Adventures: The gastronomic landscape of Marseille is still developing; in 2024, new eateries and food markets are expected to appear. Anticipate cutting-edge dining ideas that combine contemporary cuisine with classic Provençal ingredients. Improvements will also be made to the city's food markets, including Marché des Capucins and Marché de Noailles, which will now provide a greater selection of superior local goods.

In summary 2024, Marseille is expected to be a thriving and dynamic city, with many improvements and projects adding to its allure.

The city is ready to provide tourists with an even more enriched experience, from new attractions and transit upgrades to cultural events and infrastructure upgrades. In the next year, **Marseille is sure to enthrall and inspire visitors, regardless of their attraction to its natural beauty, rich cultural heritage, or historic charm.**

LOCAL INSIGHTS

Gaining a more profound and genuine understanding of Marseille may be achieved by examining the city through the perspective of its inhabitants. **These insider views capture Marseille's essence and**

highlight everything from daily activities to yearly festivals. Here, we provide first-hand accounts of events and conversations with locals that showcase Marseille's distinct charm and customs.

Interviews with Marseille Residents

Vieux Port Fisherman Jean-Luc: Could you describe your typical day in the life of a Marseille fisherman? Jean-Luc: I've spent more than 30 years fishing at Vieux Port. My day begins at three in the morning. With my team, I go out to sea, and we fish until about ten in the morning. Although we capture a range of fish, our biggest catches are anchovies and sardines. We clean and prepare the fish for the market once we get back. The fish are ready for customers and on display by midday. Although it's labor-intensive, the feeling of tradition and community here is unmatched. Fishing at the market is a social as well as a commercial endeavor.

What is your favorite thing about Marseille?

Jean-Luc: Marseille has a special vitality. It is unique because of the diversity of cultures, the stunning coastline, and the historical landmarks. I adore the cuisine, the people, and the sense of unity that permeates the whole place. Everything is constantly going on, whether it is a festival or simply a fun night out at a neighborhood café.Interview

Le Panier Artist Aline What artistic impact does Marseille have on you?

Aline: The rich cultural diversity and varied landscape of Marseille greatly influence my art. My paintings include elements such as the old buildings, the varied mix of people, and the hues of the Mediterranean. My studio is located in Le Panier, which has a creative atmosphere and winding lanes. It is like residing in a dynamic, living work of art.

Could you provide an overview of Marseille's art scene?

Aline: This place has a vibrant and diverse art scene. There are many studios and galleries, as well as a lot of artist cooperation. Street art is deeply ingrained in our culture, particularly in neighborhoods like Le Panier and Cours Julien. There is always an art festival or exhibition going on. There is a great deal of engagement between the public and artists, and the community is highly supportive.

Karim, a La Plaine restaurant owner What distinguishes the cuisine of Marseille?

Karim: The food of Marseille is a fantastic fusion of tastes from throughout the Mediterranean and beyond. We make extensive use of fresh seafood, herbs, and spices that showcase the variety of ethnic influences found in the city. **There are many North African and Italian influences,** but mainstays like bouillabaisse and aioli are also present. The focus of the cuisine is on taste and freshness.

What kind of atmosphere exists in La Plaine?

Karim: La Plaine is a colorful, artistic neighborhood. Young professionals, students, and artists all like it. There's always something going on, from street acts to live music in the pubs. With everything from fresh fruit to homemade goods, the markets are a great attraction. It's an exciting and vibrant environment, ideal for operating a restaurant.

Individual Festival Stories

The Music Day Marseille: comes alive with music on June 21st of each year for the Fête de la Musique. During this statewide event, artists from various genres play in parks, squares, and streets, transforming the whole city into one large musical space.

The Story of Isabelle: I've spent my whole life in Marseille, and one of my favorite days of the year is Fête de la Musique. My friends and I begin the evening in Vieux Port, where fantastic musicians are always performing on a large stage. After that, we explore the city, making stops to see various acts.

Discovering a jazz ensemble performing in a narrow passage in Le Panier remains one of my most treasured recollections. It was so wonderful and unexpected. The whole city seems to be celebrating together. A **fantastic evening of dancing, music, and community. Marseille FestivalEvery year, for a month-long festival of dance, music, theater, and visual arts, Marseille hosts the Festival de Marseille.** It draws artists and spectators from all over the globe with its activities and performances held in different parts of the city.

Jacques' NarrativeJacques: As a theater lover, my favorite event of the year is the Festival de Marseille. I went to a modern dance show in the outdoor Théâtre Silvain, which has a view of the sea, last summer. Both the performance and the location were magnificent. The festival's street acts and seminars are something else I like to do. It's an amazing method to encounter fresh and cutting-edge artistic expressions. The festival infuses the city with creative energy, and it's always thrilling to discover what fresh exhibitions and performances will be on offer each year.

The Suds Fiesta: Fiesta des Suds is an October festival of global music and culture. The festival offers a wide range of international performers, food vendors, art exhibits, and kid-friendly entertainment.

The Story of Marie: Our family has a custom of celebrating Fiesta des Suds. It's something we anticipate each year. With musicians from Africa, Latin America, and beyond, the music is amazing. Everyone is enjoying the performances and dancing in the electrifying environment.

We watched a great Brazilian band one year that had the whole audience up and dancing. Another feature is the food, where merchants provide international cuisine. It's a fantastic opportunity to enjoy time with family and friends while learning about other cultures.

In summary, people's tales and local knowledge provide a greater understanding of the city's distinctive customs and culture. From the colorful vibrancy of festivals to the everyday lives of artists and fishermen, these viewpoints provide an insight into what makes Marseille such a unique location.

The people of Marseille and their tales are an essential element of the city's beauty and attractiveness, **whether you're strolling through the old alleyways of Le Panier or having a wild time at Fiesta des Suds.**

MARSEILLE ITINERARY

Marseille has a diverse range of experiences to suit all kinds of visitors, regardless of how long they want to stay. To help you make the most of your stay in this energetic city, we've included a thorough schedule.

3 Days in Marseille

Seeing Marseille from the Heart Vieux Port and Le Panier in the morning begins your day in Marseille's historic center, the Vieux Port. Sip coffee at one of the numerous cafés and see the boats as they arrive and depart. Investigate the neighboring Le Panier area, which is Marseille's oldest. Explore its meandering, little streets, stop by the neighborhood stores, and take in the vibrant street art. **MuCEM and Fort Saint-Jean in the afternoon observe the European and Mediterranean Civilizations Museum (MuCEM).** The intriguing displays of Mediterranean history and culture are available at this gorgeous contemporary museum.

Walk around Fort Saint-Jean, which provides sweeping views of the city and the ocean, after seeing MuCEM. Dinner at Vieux Port in the evening savor supper at a Vieux Port seafood restaurant. Taste some regional delicacies, such as the classic fish stew bouillabaisse. Take a stroll around the dock towards the end of the evening to enjoy the lively nightlife.

Day 2: Historical and Cultural PlacesMorning: Notre Dame de la Garde BasiliqueSee the famous Basilique Notre-Dame de la Garde in Marseille. Perched on a hill, it provides stunning views of both the city and the Mediterranean. Take some time to explore the basilica, which is renowned for its exquisite interior design and spectacular architecture. La Vieille Charité and Palais Longchamp in the afternoon See the Natural History Museum and the Fine Arts Museum at Palais Longchamp, a stunning edifice. Visit La Vieille Charité at Le Panier, a stunning 17th-century almshouse that today holds museums and cultural events, after touring Palais Longchamp. Dinner at La Plaine and Cours Julien in the evening discover the artistic neighborhoods of Cours Julien and La Plaine. This neighborhood is well-known for its colorful street art, unique stores, and exciting nightlife. Savor supper at one of the several eateries serving a variety of exotic dishes.

Day 3: Unwinding in the outdoors: Calanques National Park in the morning hiking or on a boat cruise at the National Park of Calanques. It's a must-visit location for environment enthusiasts, renowned for its breathtaking limestone cliffs and turquoise seas. If you decide to trek, make sure you pack a lot of water and get going early to escape the noon heat.

Beaches and Water Sports in the Afternoon Unwind on one of Marseille's stunning beaches, such as Plage du Prado or Plage des Catalans. Try some water activities like sailing, snorkeling, or scuba diving if you're feeling daring. Dinner at La Corniche in the evening makes your way to La Corniche for a supper al fresco. This charming seaside road has a lot of eateries with breathtaking views of the ocean. Savor a leisurely supper while taking in the sunset over the Mediterranean, maybe even sipping some local wines.

A Week in MarseilleDay 1-3

Following the 3-Day Itinerary With the three-day schedule above, you can cover the must-see attractions and events in Marseilles to start your week off well.

Day 4: Tour of Aix-en-Provence for the DayDaybreak and Evening: Look around Aix-en-ProvenceTravel to Aix-en-Provence, a little town renowned for its stunning architecture and lively markets, by taking a quick train journey. **See the major avenue, Cours Mirabeau, which is dotted with cafés, fountains, and trees.** Discover the Saint-Sauveur Cathedral and the Musée Granet, which has pieces by renowned painters like Cézanne.Evening: Go back to MarseilleIn the evening, go back to Marseille and have a leisurely meal at a neighborhood eatery.

Day 5: Immersion in Culture: Breakfast at Château d'IfTake a boat trip to Château d'If, a castle that has been converted into a jail and made well-known by Alexandre Dumas' book **"The Count of Monte Cristo."**Discover the fascinating history of the stronghold and the island as you explore them.

Afternoon: Museums and Art: See the Marseille History Museum for a thorough examination of the history of the city. Visit the Friche la Belle de Mai, a cultural complex with galleries, workshops, and performance spaces, to learn about modern art.

Evening: Nightlife and Live MusicVisit a jazz club or live music venue in Marseille. Locations such as Le Molotov and Espace Julien provide outstanding shows. Savor the exciting nightlife in communities such as Vieux Port and La Plaine.

Day 6: Wine Tours and Luberon Villages: Sunrise and Sunset: Luberon VillagesVisit the charming Luberon villages, such as Bonnieux, Roussillon, and Gordes, by car or on a guided trip. Explore the quaint neighborhoods, go to the markets, and take in the breathtaking Provençal landscape.

Afternoon: Tours of Wine: Take a wine-tasting trip at a nearby vineyard. Provence is renowned for producing top-notch wines, particularly rosé. Taste a variety of regional wines and discover the process of creating wine.

Evening: Go back to Marseille back to Marseille and have a laid-back evening. Think of having dinner in a classic French restaurant.

Day 7: Unwinding and visiting local markets: Park Borély in the morning Visit Parc Borély, a stunning public park including gardens, a lake, and a château, and enjoy a relaxing morning there. Take a boat out on the lake, rent a bike, or just kick back with a picnic.

Local Markets in the **Afternoon:** Take a look at the Marché de Noailles, a thriving marketplace that sells regional specialties, spices, and fresh food.

Discover the Marché des Capucins, a bustling market renowned for its assortment of food vendors and welcoming ambiance.

Evening: Dinner of Farewell: Savor a goodbye meal in a classy Marseille restaurant. Think about making a reservation at the Michelin-starred Le Petit Nice, which serves delicious fish meals. Enjoy your last evening in this fascinating city as you look back on your week spent in Marseille.

In summary: Marseille is a city that skillfully combines its natural beauty, culture, and history. There is a lot to see and do whether you have a few days or a whole week to spend there. Marseille provides a wide variety of activities that suit all interests, from discovering historic strongholds and lively districts to indulging in top-notch food and breathtaking coastline vistas. **Make the most of your trip and lose yourself in the distinct charm of this Mediterranean treasure by following this schedule.**

CONCLUSION

Every visitor's heart and imagination are captivated by Marseille. Marseille is a location that will never be forgotten because of its remarkable historical tapestry and breathtaking seaside vistas.

Final Thoughts on Marseille

Marseille is an experience rather than merely a place. Situated on the shore of the Mediterranean, it has been a cultural melting pot for more than 2,600 years. Travelers of all stripes should not miss this energetic port city, which combines attractions from antiquity with contemporary culture.

The Allure of Vieux Port: Marseille's center is the Vieux Port, often known as the Old Port. Since ancient times, this busy port has served as a hub for trade and business. These days, it's a bustling neighborhood with markets, cafés, and seafood restaurants. The everyday sight of the fisherman selling their catch of the day adds to the allure of this ancient harbor

.

Cultural and Historic Treasures: Numerous historical and cultural attractions may be found in Marseille. **Situated on a hill, the Basilique Notre-Dame de la Garde is a landmark of the city,** providing sweeping views of Marseille. Explore the cultural history of the Mediterranean at the Museum of European and Mediterranean Civilizations (MuCEM), and stroll through the old Le Panier quarter, which has galleries and artisan stores tucked away along its winding, small alleyways.

Natural beauty: The stunning splendor of nature envelops Marseille. Hiking and boating are ideal at the Calanques National Park, which has breathtaking cliffs and blue seas. With its fine sands and crystal-clear, swimming-friendly waters, beaches like Plage des Catalans and Plage du Prado provide a tranquil haven from the bustle of the city.

Gourmet Treats: Marseille's varied background is reflected in its food scene. Local favorites include the delicious fish stew bouillabaisse and the garlic mayonnaise aïoli. There is no shortage of seafood, with many recipes heavily using fresh catches. Don't pass up the opportunity to eat at one of the numerous eateries in the lively districts or near the waterfront.

Your Next Adventure

It's time to plan your next trip as your time in Marseille draws to an end. Whether your goal is to go to a new location or see more of France, here are some intriguing possibilities to think about

Wine Tour of Provence: Not too far from Marseille lies the wine-producing area of Provence. Enjoy wine tastings, go on a guided tour of the vineyards, and discover how wine is made.

Domaine de la Brillane and Château La Coste are a few of the well-known wineries. Château La Coste Address: 13610 Le Puy-Sainte-Réparade, France; 2750 Route de la Cridecontact@chateau-la-coste.com via email

Cost: Individual tours begin at €20.Address: 2626 Route de Puyricard, 13540 Aix-en-Provence, France; Domaine de la **Brillane Contact:** contact@domainedelabrillane.com via emailWine tastings start at €10 per person.

See the Villages of Luberon: The Luberon area is well known for its quaint hilltop towns, such Bonnieux, Roussillon, and Gordes. These settlements provide breathtaking vistas, a glimpse of traditional Provençal life, and ancient architecture. Local travel companies depart from Marseille for day visits. Provence Panorama Tours **Contact:** contact@provence-panorama.com

Address: 7 Rue Joseph Vernet, 84000 Avignon, **1 France Price:** Day excursions begin at €100 per person.

Th1e Palais des Papes and Avignon: trip into the past may be had by visiting Avignon, which is well-known for the Palais des Papes, a **UNESCO World Heritage site**. The popes lived in this enormous Gothic castle throughout the fourteenth century. From Marseille, it takes around one hour by rail to get to Avignon.Palais des Papes

Address: 84000 Avignon, France; Place du PalaisContact palais-des-papes.com via email.

Cost: Each entry fee is around €12.

The Roman History of Arles
Arles: is renowned for both its association with Vincent van Gogh and its beautifully preserved Roman monuments. See the Alyscamps Necropolis, the Roman Amphitheater, and the Ancient Theater. Rencontres d'Arles, a famous photography event, is also held in Arles. Les Arènes d'Arles Email: info@arenes-arles.com

Address: Rond-Point des Arènes, 13200 Arles, France

Cost: Each entry fee is approximately €9.

The Calanques and Cassis: The charming fishing hamlet of Cassis is the starting point for seeing the breathtaking Calanques, and it's just a short drive from Marseille. Discover these stunning limestone cliffs and undiscovered coves by boat tour.

Contact: contact@cassis-calanques-tours.com Address: Quai des Baux, 13260 Cassis, FrancePrice: Boat trips cost between €20 and €30 per person.6. The Camargue Natural Park Discover the distinctive topography of the Camargue, an area renowned for its pink flamingos, wild horses, and marshes. Take a guided safari excursion or ride a horse to explore the region. The Camargue is renowned for producing salt and rice.

Email: info@camargue-safari-tours.com Address: 5 Rue des Flamants Roses, 13460 Saintes-Maries-de-la-Mer, **FrancePrice:** The first ticket is €50 per person.

Organizing Your Upcoming Journey: Think back to your favorite aspects of Marseille when you plan your next vacation, and seek for comparable experiences in other locations. France and its surrounding regions provide a multitude of experiences, whether it is in the areas of history, nature, or food. Buses and trains are practical and effective modes of transportation. Hiring a vehicle may also be a terrific opportunity to go at your speed around the countryside and to more isolated locations.

Final Thoughts: Marseille is a city that makes a lasting impact. **Its rich history, cultural variety, and natural beauty make it a location worth returning to again and again.** From the old alleyways of Le Panier to the contemporary attractions of MuCEM, Marseille provides a unique experience that blends the best of both worlds. **Cherish the memories of Marseille's hospitality, delectable food, and breathtaking scenery as you reflect on your stay.**

Marseille provides experiences that you'll remember forever, whether you're dining at a neighborhood bistro, **visiting the Calanques, or taking in the sunset over the Vieux Port.** The purpose of travel is to connect and explore. Every adventure broadens your perspective on the world and how you fit within it. Thus, never stop learning, maintain your curiosity, and welcome the experiences that lie ahead. **Good luck on your journey!**

FREQUENTLY ASKED QUESTIONS

There are generally a **lot of questions while visiting a new place.** To assist you in making travel plans and guarantee a seamless and pleasurable experience, we answer some of the most often-asked concerns about visiting Marseille right here.

What time of year is ideal for travel to Marseille?

The ideal seasons to visit Marseille are from **April to June** in the spring and from September to November in the autumn when there are fewer tourists and nice weather. Although it may be quite hot and busy, summer (**July and August)** is also a terrific time to enjoy sunny weather and exciting events. Because winter **(December to February)** is mild, it's an excellent time to go on a budget or if you'd rather stay alone.

What is the route to Marseille?

In response, Marseille is accessible by car, rail, plane, and sea:

By Air: There are several domestic and international flights from Marseille-Provence Airport (MRS), which is located around 27 kilometers (17 miles) from the city center.

By rail: High-speed trains (TGV) link Marseille's principal rail station, Gare de Marseille Saint-Charles, to major cities in France and Europe.

Via Car: Marseille has excellent highway access. By automobile, it takes around seven hours from Paris.

By Sea: Ferries from North Africa, Sardinia, and Corsica arrive at Marseille's port.

Which kind of transportation works best in Marseille?

In response, Marseille provides a range of transit choices:

Public Transportation: The RTM network runs a metro system, buses, and trams.

Taxis and Ride-Sharing: The city offers ride-sharing services via applications like Uber.

Walking and Biking: Walking is a terrific way to explore districts like Le Panier and Vieux Port, while biking is permitted in Marseille with several rental alternatives.

Is it safe for visitors visiting Marseille?

Yes, travelers may feel comfortable visiting Marseille most of the time. Like in any big city, it's best to exercise care and be alert, particularly in congested places. Steer clear of dimly lit, empty locations after dark, and keep **an eye out for pickpockets in popular tourist destinations.**

Which sights in Marseille are a must-see?

In response, one of Marseille's main attractions is Vieux Port: The region around the old port. **The Basilique Notre-Dame de la Garde** provides expansive city vistas. The Museum of European and Mediterranean Civilizations, or MuCEM, is a cutting-edge institution with outstanding displays. **Marseille's oldest neighborhood, Le Panier District, with quaint lanes and artisan stores.** Château d'If: Well-known stronghold and former jail situated on a bay island.

Which foods should you eat in Marseille?

In response, Marseille is renowned for its extensive gastronomic history. One food you should try is **Bouillabaisse:** A classic stew made with fish. Aioli: Fish is often served with garlic mayonnaise.Pastis: An alcohol with an anise taste.Navettes: Biscuits with an orange taste.

Where in Marseille can I locate inexpensive lodging?

There are affordable lodging options accessible all across Marseille. Choices consist of Budget tourists often choosing hostels.

Low-cost Hotels: There are a lot of these hotels all across the city.

Vacation Rentals: Websites such as Airbnb provide affordable accommodations.

Which activities in Marseille are suitable for families?

Marseille has a plethora of family-friendly activities.

Aquariums and Zoos: The Natural History Museum at Palais Longchamp and the Parc Animalier de la Barben are two examples.

Parks and Playgrounds: Children will love Parc Chanot and Parc Borély.Children-Friendly Museums: Interactive displays may be seen in the Marseille History Museum and MuCEM.

How can I get a taste of Marseille culture?

To get fully immersed in the culture of the area: Visit markets and have a look at the Marché du Prado and de Noailles.

Attend Festivals: The lively culture of the city is on display during occasions like the Festival de Marseille.

Discover Neighborhoods: To get a taste of the local way of life, take a stroll around Le Panier and Cours Julien.

What is the best place for LGBTQ+ tourists to go in Marseille?

Yes, LGBTQ+ tourists are welcome in Marseille. **The city has pubs, events, and places that are welcoming to LGBTQ+ people, such as the Marseille Pride Parade.** Resources for safety and assistance are easily accessible.

What is appropriate local etiquette and tradition knowledge?

Answer: Being aware of local traditions can improve your visit.

Greetings: Friends may give each other cheek kisses as well as a brief handshake.

Dining etiquette: Don't begin your meal until after everyone has been served.

Tipping: Although not required, leaving a modest gratuity (5–10%) at restaurants is appreciated.

What are Marseille's emergency phone numbers?

In response, the following emergency numbers are crucial:

Police: 17

Fire Department: Eighteen15 Ambulance Services AvailableEmergency Number in Europe: 112

Is there a credit card machine in Marseille?

The majority of stores in Marseille take credit cards, but it's always a good idea to have cash on hand for smaller purchases and markets. There are plenty of ATMs across the whole city.

How can I exchange money and what is the local currency?

The Euro (€) is the currency used locally. Banks, airports, and specialized exchange bureaus all provide currency exchange services. You may easily take out euros straight from your bank account using ATMs.

In what way is Marseille accessible to tourists with disabilities?

The city of Marseille is becoming more and more accessible to tourists with impairments. **Wheelchair-accessible hotels,** popular tourist destinations, and public transportation all provide amenities. It's a good idea to confirm accessible features when making travel and lodging arrangements, especially when visiting certain locations.

Which language is spoken in Marseille, and is French a prerequisite?

The majority language used is French. Even though English is widely spoken by residents in tourist regions, knowing a few simple French words might improve your experience. The following are some helpful words: Hi there: Hello!

Regards and thanks: Thank you would you please: If you would please you be able to speak English? Do you speak English?

In Marseille, how can I maintain my connection?

Remaining in touch is simple: Wi-Fi is widely accessible in public spaces, hotels, and cafés.

SIM Cards: Get a local SIM card from companies such as Bouygues Telecom, Orange, or SFR. Check about roaming packages while traveling abroad by contacting your home operator.

Do guided trips departing from Marseille exist?

In-depth explanations of the history and culture of the city may be obtained via guided tours, which are offered. There are other options, such as boat cruises to Château d'If and the Calanques, bike tours, and walking tours. **Numerous experiences catered** to various interests are available from local tour providers.

What travel essentials should I bring to Marseille?

In response, some packing necessities are Sturdy walking shoes: For city exploration.

Weather-appropriate attire: summertime sun protection and light layers for the spring and autumn. Use a travel adapter to charge your electronics. Swimsuit: For lounging on the beaches and engaging in water sports.

How can I book lodging and attractions in advance?

In most cases, reservations may be made online using official websites or platforms like TripAdvisor**, Airbnb, and Booking.com.** For reservations, visit the official websites of the individual attractions. Making reservations in advance is advised, particularly during the busiest travel seasons.

We strive to offer you a thorough idea of what to anticipate and how to prepare for your trip to Marseille by answering some often-asked questions.
Enjoy your time in this beautiful and ancient city!
HAPPY TRAVELS !